little landslides

how we RISE UP
from our PAIN

DR. BRIDGET COOPER

~2017~

Melanie,

May your little

landslides place you

on blessed ground!

Peace,

Bridget

ISBN-13: 978-0692813003
ISBN-10: 069813004

DEDICATION

This book is dedicated to my daughters,

Jessica & Elena.

May you gracefully welcome the pains you face,

joyfully transforming them into something majestic

with your wisdom, strength, and enduring love.

CONTENTS

TRIBUTES

"Believe you can and you're halfway there."
~ Theodore Roosevelt

This book, in all its darkness, is grounded in light.

My light bearers are many and all lovely in how they've shone the way for me to be able to complete this labor of love. Living through these stories the first time almost shattered me. Crawling back up inside myself to live – and tell about – them again was, well, unpleasant. Yet, I knew it would bring healing to the world and a voice to those still mute so I dove head-first into the abyss. Without this list of people, I know I wouldn't have emerged as calm, clear, and soft as I did.

First and foremost, to my miraculous, beautiful, and badass daughters, Jessica & Elena: If my life is based only on my ability to protect you from the harm I experienced, I hope I have been successful. One thing I've learned along the winding road is that my job is to equip you to face down any demon you meet with insight, grace, and a shit ton of boundaries. I pray I've helped to solidly build those things in you. You are my life's greatest joy and honor and I pray to be by your side for as many of your little landslides as life will allow. I sincerely hope you won't read this book until you're much older than you are now, as the stories about your mommy are gripping and I don't want these shadow figures in your tender hearts.

To Grandma Dor: Here's the book you've been waiting for. Well, the first edition, anyway. I'm so grateful for our bond, for the mirror you held to me in some of my darkest and brightest times. You reminded me in so many ways not to squander a minute of the precious time we have here. I love and miss you, yet I feel you here with me every step of my delicious journey.

To Lisa: Yeah, I did it. I finally did it. I stepped out into the light and showed up as my honest, twisted, broken, and put-back- together-again self. I'm glad that I don't know a world without your friendship. We may not have been born sisters but we sure as hell are going to leave this world as them. When I'm sitting under that famous oak tree, I'm going to reserve a "I told you so" giggle just for you, with my phoenix tattoo in full view.

To Auntie Joanie: I was so very afraid to have you read this book, knowing that a person you loved abundantly was forefront in my abuse story. I am so grateful for your compassion, support, and honesty as this book took shape. I've been blessed to have you in my world, as my cheerleader, my guide, and my confidante. I love you to the moon and back.

To Kelly, my talented cover designer: You handled the pressure I put on you like a champ! This was a unique beast and I'm so grateful for your willingness to see my vision and help it come to life. Thank you for being my designated and committed "Cover Lover." (lol)

To Kimberly T., my talented photographer. Thank you for jumping in and helping me to cast the vision of this book onto film. Your patience, reassurance, and confidence in me made a tough process so much easier (and fun!). You have unparalleled style and I'm blessed to call you my friend.

To Kim S.: Once again, I'm so grateful for your behind-the-scenes encouragement. You were always there, seeking out opportunities to listen to me as I wrestled this book down into its final form. As you confront the darkest hallways in your own life, I hope you'll recall the courage you summoned in me and sprinkle that shit everywhere to illuminate your path. Thank you for being my friend.

To Kimberlea: Thank you for reminding me of the value of story. You inspired me to speak my truth and stay grounded along the way. As part of my Goddess Circle, you strengthen me each and every day with your grace and peaceful way.

To the clients and colleagues who have turned to me over the years for my guidance over the years: Thank you for allowing me the honor to walk with you on your healing journey. I hope that this book continues our conversations and that you'll pass it along to another who needs the light.

To my advance reviewers: I feel blessed to have had such bold and daring souls cross my path. I trusted you with my most vulnerable of stories and the care you showed them touched my soul. Thank you for taking the time and energy to read my manuscript and share your insights and reflections. Without your encouragement, I may never have put this into print. From the bottom of my heart, thank you.

To my Badass Brigade: What would this book (and my spirit) be without my legion of strong, willing, courageous, and loving extended circle of supporters around the globe. How did this girl get so damn lucky? Thank you for pushing me to stand boldly in my light so that I could shine it for those still in the darkness.

To my abusers – those I loved and those I barely knew – thank you for sending me so far down so that I could know pain, and for getting out of my way so that I could rise up and experience what true grit looks like. I was born a badass and although your inner pain projected outward and onto my tender shoulders threatened to destroy me, I overcame. Without you, I might have lived a bland, ordinary life. I like this spicy, extraordinary life much better anyway, thank you very much. May you know peace in this life and the one(s) hereafter.

To you, the reader: I genuinely applaud your courage to read this book. I know the subject matter is raw and graphic and downright painful at times. I pray that you'll find a part of yourself that is in pain now, healed. Please don't let anyone's harm continue to weigh you down; you're better than that. My Badass Warrior of Love & Light motto: *Do no harm but take no shit.*

To little Bridget: In diving head-first into the mud of my painful past, I honor myself, my experience, my stumbles, and my victories. I wrote this book to honor you and all of the things you've been through and the times you've been face down in the mud, not sure if you could get back up. I testify to this: You were not meant to stay in the mud. Like the lotus, you come from mud but crave, and deserve, the sunlight. No mud, no lotus.

This book serves a return to myself. To reveal and honor all of the broken pieces of myself, some which have healed and some which continue to challenge me. To demonstrate that healing is possible. That joy shines through pain. That forgiveness is transformational. The power over your life is yours and yours alone to wield.

"There will always be people in your life who treat you wrong. Be sure to thank them for making you strong." ~ Zig Ziglar

CONTEXT

"You are never too old to be
what you might have been. " ~ George Eliot

Having just finished this book amidst the 2016 presidential election, I reflected that it couldn't have happened at a better time. There's a cacophony of voices in our world right now, battling over human rights, leadership, and our individual and collective morality. What will we allow? What can we withstand?

The 2016 election season triggered me in powerful, transformative ways. I'm one of those "pick myself up and move on" sort of women and I really thought that my abusive past was behind me. When I saw footage of our now president-elect on stage, I quickly realized how very wrong I was to think so. Watching him in the presidential debates, I experienced a post-traumatic reaction, literally shaking as I sat watching him pace, linger, hover, and seethe. Although twenty years (and some DNA) separate them, my body was thoroughly convinced that this man was my ex-husband.

So many women have posted on social media this shared experience. Why? He is an amalgam of the abusive, controlling, raging men we've encountered and had to run or hide from or rise above our entire lives. Misogyny is a real thing; and now, it's taken the form of a world leader.

He's going to be our *president*.

With that said, I still cannot fully comprehend what so many marginalized members of our society are feeling after this ugly election season. I cannot tackle all of the social injustices here, but I do feel them just the same.

To address the "female" part of this, what's been missed by so many is that this has never been about vulgarity or bad language. Although I do expect decorum and class from a world leader, I don't care if he says "pussy" all day long. If he wants to say "fuck" 10,000 times a day (off camera, I hope), he can be my guest.

What **do** I care about? Him bragging about grabbing women's bodies and feeling entitled to do so because of his position and wealth.

That is beyond wrong. Sadly, it's what happens every hour of every day. Whether you want to face it or not, there are a great number of men who feel entitled to women's bodies. It falls beyond the line of objectification where women's value is placed largely on their looks and sexual function. It's the dirty little secret that has now become mainstage thanks to our President-Elect: Many men, especially those with power, think that women were born to submit to men and their desires, particularly if they perceive that we are "guilty" of drawing their desire forth. If we are attractive or friendly or sexy, we are blamed for our enticing prowess.

Those of us who have been sexually assaulted, victims of domestic violence, and persecuted due to national origin, religion, sexual orientation, etc. tended to feel differently about this election. When almost half of the voters stood in support of a person who not only doesn't take these matters seriously but brags, mocks, and supports the abuse, it's a troubling, terrifying, and hugely upsetting message.

The rhetoric about crying and whining about a "loss" served to underscore the injury. Women and others who have been abused, violated, and marginalized are inclined to see this election as dismissive of our experience. Many of us have been told to "just move on" after this election, yet those are the same words we heard after we were assaulted by those who couldn't or wouldn't find a way to stand for us.

"It's not such a big deal." "You didn't die." "You weren't injured." "At least you didn't get pregnant." "Can you really consider it rape? You were dating." Personally, I was told that "boys will be boys" after I was assaulted at the age of 11 and I heard the same thing in this election in the infamous "locker room" defense.

Like a great deal of people, when I woke to learn the election outcome, it took my breath away. My younger daughter, almost thirteen, had gone to bed while Florida and Virginia were ominously flip flopping between the two front runners. Like me, she was eternally hopeful that he wouldn't win. My older daughter is gay and was floored to hear that he won. Even now, I don't even want to type his name so I'll refer to the pronoun instead. Let's be clear: I was not in support of Clinton and neither were my daughters. This wasn't about being pro-Hillary. This was simply and purely about being against him.

According to the pollsters, this election was, in part, about change. That's how those who voted for him substantiated their vote. I want political, economic, and social change, too. As a self-employed single mother, I pay out the nose for my health insurance. Career politicians, special interest groups, and big money driving our political system makes me uneasy and revolted with the buying of elections and political decisions.

To overlook everything else and vote for him to try to send a message about change is what deeply concerned me. This isn't reality television. The likelihood that he will be able to make meaningful change is far-fetched. He campaigned on fear, anger, and hopelessness. He never expected to win, but those base human emotions catapulted him into the White House. Dark draws in the darkness to create more. And it did.

As I processed all of this with friends and colleagues, I equated this election process to labor and delivery. Having had both of my children without pain medication, I can tell you that labor and delivery is quite painful. As painful as my first labor and delivery was, I happily embarked on getting pregnant again to do it all over. Why? Because I was able to forget the pain almost as soon as it ended because I was holding a beautiful baby in my arms.

When this election put him into office, there was no sweet, cooing baby to lull us into sweet oblivion. There were no sighs of relief that the pain was over. No, my friends, the pain has just begun. We cannot forget the wounds that were ripped open on the campaign trail because they are still bleeding.

With that said, what now? How can we get through and past all of this?

I've read so many courageous and peaceful social media posts by people trying to process how they feel and where they'll go from here. Sadly, just like when we are assaulted or abused directly, it becomes our job to figure out how to "deal."

How We Rise Up From Our Pain

Just like I did with my abusers, I've become squarely focused on my gratitude for how they have changed me through challenge. I've actually found myself thanking Donald Trump (there, I said his name) for peeling back the shroud cast over the latent anger and resentment that comprised a great deal of this vote. This election has provided an opportunity for us to educate, enlighten, heal, and grow. No oppressor will determine my joy and the trajectory of my life, including this presidency. I vow to rise higher, brighter, and stronger. I vow to not let a predator – even if he holds our great nation's highest office – define my joy, my love, my freedom, and my FUTURE. I cannot reclaim my past but I absolutely get to own my future.

Part of that future for me needs to include mending fences. Perpetuating a divide isn't how I was built so I must be true to my nature. I teach heart-centered conflict resolution so I've been doing my best to practice what I preach as my Facebook feed has been bombarded with political threads, especially the post-election ones. The key to any successful discussion is the willingness and capacity to see the world through another person's experience of it. I work with people a great deal on mental models and unpacking them so they can see their choice in holding them as "truth." Honestly, I don't feel warm and fuzzy when I think of talking to a die-hard Trump supporter since I have built my own mental model about how far apart we are on how we see the world and the solutions to solve problems we face. Consistent with my conflict resolution approach, you have to start with agreement and ask, "Where is our shared outlook or experience?"

In this situation I'm certain that we share one thing: Pain. The vast majority of those who voted for Trump did so because he represented change. Why would anyone want change? To ease pain or discomfort. So "they" are in pain and so are we....that's our starting point. I am called to see our shared pain, acknowledge it, find its true source, and find ways to ease it.

Politicians feed off of our pain, promising us a salve to our burns yet they rarely deliver. This election caused so much pain for so many people that it's apropos that we direct our energies at easing it. The other rampant emotion is fear. There is so much fear. Fear emanates from a lack of control over future events. I've witnessed so many plans springing from this fear, actions that put their doers in the driver's seat. From organizing marches and protests to contributing their time and money to threatened charities. From posting words of support to fearful members of our society to engaging in enlightening dialogue with the opposition. Taking some form of action makes us feel more in control and therefore less fearful.

Me? I wrote a book about my experiences to give voice to my *pain* and my *rising*.

What can you do? What action can you take? What bridge can you build and cross? When others threaten to destroy, build. When others promise to injure, heal. In the famous words of Martin Luther King, Jr.:

"Darkness cannot cast out darkness. Only light can do that."

Be the light.

~ Dr. B

"Most of the shadows of life are caused by standing in our own sunshine." ~ Ralph Waldo Emerson

Warning:

If you are deeply empathetic and/or you have a personal abuse history, I've been told that this subject matter is profoundly disturbing. Before you dive in, identify some ways you'll take care of yourself as you read the book and some people you can reach out to for comfort and support. These might be friends or these might be professionals (therapist, support group, etc.). The important thing is that you get the support you need if this subject matter hits you in dark places.

WHY

"An unconsidered life
is not one worth living." ~ Socrates

A photo of a baby, beaten and bloody at the hands of his babysitter, circulated in May of 2016 on social media (if you're curious, look up "Marbury family from Oregon"), apparently beaten by his caretaker. Tragically, because of some arcane law in that state, the abuser couldn't be prosecuted because the baby couldn't testify that the injuries were intentional. The baby was *clearly* and horrifically abused but the abuser would never be held liable or accountable. The abuser would get away with what he'd done to that innocent child.

I could hardly breathe.

I knew that I was looking into a time-lapsed mirror, one that brought me back to moments I couldn't recollect but knew in my bones.

The body remembers what the mind wishes to forget.

I was that baby, many, many, many times. My face bruised, swollen, and scarred. My eyes vacant and fearful. My mind trying to make sense of the nonsensical. People I loved causing me devastating pain and terror.

1

~

After an abnormal psychology class lecture one winter night during my sophomore year in college, I asked my professor, "what would happen to a child if she was raped and beaten before she had conscious memory?"

His response? "She would never get past that. She would have no hope of recovery. The wounds would absolutely destroy her."

No hope of recovery.

Absolutely destroyed.

Well, Mr. Professor, thank you for your prediction (and the inherent dare you offered to prove you wrong), but, *kiss my ass*. Those wounds *didn't* destroy me. If anything, they made me stronger, smarter, and more loving. They made me fierce. They made me tender and rock solid.

They made me *me*.

To right that wrong, that hope Mr. Professor Man ripped from my spirit, I feel compelled to show you how to break free of the curse, one that my professor thought was impenetrable. In order to do that, I'll need to share my story.

~

Everyone has a story.

We connect over stories. We come together over stories.

We see ourselves and those we love in stories.

How We Rise Up From Our Pain

We draw parallels in stories.

We gain insight, inspiration, and understanding through stories.

We deepen our empathy and build our resolve through stories.

This book contains mine.

My little landslides, my triumphs and devastations, all entwined together in the stories that formed the path of my life, that delivered me into my professional calling. (For those Fleetwood Mac fans out there, yes, their song is playing in my head every time I reflect on the title of this book.) I've been on the receiving (and giving) end of a host of pains, challenges, heartbreaks, victories, and losses: *My* little landslides.

Landslides are known as overwhelmingly positive ("won by a landslide") and horribly negative ("the village was wiped out by a landslide"). This book demonstrates both. My rapid downward movements and my overwhelming victories despite – and because of – the things that threatened to destroy me. I chronicle the formative ones in this book. I also share how these landslides did what landslides do: Formed a new landscape, a new foundation on which to rise from.

The purpose of this book is to *provide hope*. To show you a way through and out. Hope for a better, more peaceful, connected, joyful life. One that you were born deserving. New ground on the remnants of the old.

Life hands us some pretty raw deals and hope eludes us when it's what we need the most. I struggled for years to find a reason to hold onto hope. It wasn't until someone else saw my massive scars, felt my enormous pain, and reflected back that a new way of living was possible that I was able to shift from the old to the new patterning.

I want to be *that* for *you*.

~ The Nuts and Bolts ~

I'm starting my story at the end to get to the beginning. It shares the story of my ruin, and the path to my salvation. An author friend, the illustrious Ann Sheybani, advised me to define a "container" for my stories, a span or theme that encompasses them so that they don't just ramble on without a clear purpose. Choosing my time span was easy: It's the period between my birth and midway through my eighteenth year. Why? Because the outer point of that container marked the first time I faced my demons and decided to live, to face them no matter how painful, to find recovery and healing, to end the pain instead of trying to end my life.

There's a quote traveling around social media that says some version of "be kind to others because you never know what battles they are fighting." This book aims to give a front row seat to that truth. If you met me after I conducted a seminar, gave a keynote, or facilitated a staff retreat, you'd likely conclude that I've been blessed with a pretty mundane life, sprinkled here and there with some challenge like we all do.

Like many of us, I don't wear my scars on the outside. If you take me at face value, you'll never know the source of my compassion, my deep love, my intensity and passion for life and healing, and my profound sensitivity to all things, particularly humanity. You'd skate right past those, making assumptions about any number of things to fit with your world view. That's not an indictment in any way; it's what we do.

See yourself as the
full, glorious,
torn and sewn,
ripped and repaired,
soiled and cleansed
quilt of human
pleasure and pain
that you are.

Sharing my stories, my "why" for committing my life to the work that I do, serves to lift the veil. In that vein, I pray that you will do will do the same for your own life. Get real honest so you can be the real you.

I'm not your typical woman so this book is anything but typical. It's not simply a memoir, nor is it simply a self-help guide. It's both. I'm going to tell you my story, how my spirit got ripped apart in every imaginable way very early in life. The story chapters are told in the first person, sharing a vignette about something that marked my journey. At times, I layer one story on top of another, using time and location headings to alert you to that shift. I'll offer you some context along the way so that you can understand more fully where *those* stories fits into the fabric of *my* story.

The events depicted in this book are real, true, and often graphic. Some are direct from my memory, things a chemical fire couldn't remove from my synapses. Others are pieced together from what my mom told me when I was a child. I meditated before each of these writing sessions, wanting to gracefully and intentionally open the authentic pathway to those core memories. Originally intending to use *some* creative license to bring some of my earliest experiences to life from a first-person perspective, I was floored by how easily the words came pouring through my fingers, like I was tapping into a memory bank long-buried.

I pray that I've done them justice.

At the end of the book, after all the stories have been told, I'll do what I do best: Advise. I'll put my professional hat on and I'll offer a roadmap for recovering from whatever stories, burdens, hurts, and scars you're holding so you can be free.

Freedom. Ohhhh, yes. I want that for you more than anything.

Why? I don't even know you! Yet, my "why" is easy: Because we share this beautiful planet and we keep destroying it and each other because we are hurt and angry and disconnected and we've either forgotten or never learned how to love very well. I want more than that for *you* and for *us*. There's a better way, regardless of the pain you've experienced. You don't believe me? Read on...I will inspire and teach you how to rise up, above and beyond the weights you have latched to your ankles.

But first, please do me a favor: Take a deep, cleansing breath. Get inside your body. Feel your fingertips. Wiggle your toes. Be present and real and connected to this book – this moment – or it's not going to do you a damned bit of good. Own this opportunity to *feel* what I'm about to tell you. In order to do that, you'll need to open up your heart a little. If you stay in your head you'll miss its gift, its power. And it has power to give to you.

Speaking of power, take note of the symbol that starts each chapter; in Chinese, it means "strength." This book is firmly grounded in it, paying tribute to the tenacious and formidable nature of the human spirit.

In this case, mine.

"Our job is not to deny the story but to defy the ending
to rise strong, recognize our story, and
rumble with the truth until we get to a place where we think,
'yes, this is what happened. This is my truth and
I will choose how this story ends.'"~ Brene Brown

CHAPTER ONE

CLOSET

力

Amherst, Massachusetts
1989, Age 18

I cannot *believe* it's the last night of classes before finals. After finals, I'll move off campus for the winter break so I can avoid going home. Anything but that.

I must have tried on three different outfits already and nothing is working. I feel like a fat cow in everything. At 5'3" and 125 pounds, I literally thunder as I make my way down the dorm hall. I'm disgusting. My thighs are immense. People are looking at me, wondering how I let myself get this out of control? I can hear their thoughts piercing my stressed mind. "She's gross. Who would ever want HER? What a pitiful mess!" I'm eighteen and I've already been written off by the world.

Outside, frigid wind is whipping between the towering buildings at UMass Amherst. I bundle up, adding bulk to my flabbiness by sporting long underwear beneath my loose cotton pants. I couldn't feel fatter even if I duct tape actual blubber to my legs.

I can't leave the dorm. I need to get to class soon but I can't have anyone see me looking like this. People will stare. I'll be humiliated. They will see me for who I really am: A shameful disaster.

I can feel the panic washing over me. My breathing is getting tight. I'm suffocating. My head is spinning, full of thoughts I can't control. The laughter and buzz of my floor mates fills the hallway, like a party I wasn't invited to. I've got to get out of here, yet I have to hide.

The service elevator at the end of the hallway calls to me like a lighthouse beacon. The fact that I'm claustrophobic doesn't stop me from breaking my way into that contraption like Indiana Jones' search for the Holy Grail. I need relief from the noise, the clamor. I need to hide from the world, from myself. Clueless as to the roadmap for that, I press the button and enter its inner sanctum.

I find it almost funny that I'm locking myself in an enclosed space given how incredibly, paralyzing-ly claustrophobic I am. I can't stand being in small rooms, let alone elevators. My mind wanders back to a shed, and the day I once felt the walls closing in on me.

~

Mission Hills, California
1975, Age 4

It's one of those bright days where you seek refuge from the blaze before it burns you. I'm three, maybe four, at a daycare center in the outskirts of Los Angeles. There are some older kids with us, big boys, and I'm not sure why.

Playing in the dusty yard, sparse with a few toys and swings and things, I'm led by those boys to a small shed in the corner of the yard. The boys tell me that we are there to play house. The din in the yard veils our wanderings; so many voices and so much movement to attend to.

We enter the shed.

It's so tight in there with four of us. Or are there five? My senses are overwhelmed. There's a wooden table in the center of the room, some sort of crafting table, a place where things get created or fixed. They chant for me to get up on the table. I clamber up there, awkwardly, trying not to look careless in my pretty dress.

Mommy will be mad if I get it dirty or ripped. We don't have much money. I know this because Mommy tells me all the time how scared she is that we won't have a place to live soon.

It's just her and me.

She works so hard. That's why I'm here, so she can work so hard. If Mommy doesn't work, it's bad. Bad things happen when Mommy worries. She drinks and smokes those funny cigarettes and cries a lot. I make her smile when I smile so I smile a lot.

Today, I'm wearing one of my favorite dresses, a short cotton little thing with bright flowers. I love this dress. And I have my frilly, white ankle socks and my shiny black Mary Janes. I could be going to church in this outfit, if we went to church.

Instead, I'm in this oversized closet, stuffed with boys. But I feel so pretty, so free. When we were in the yard I could feel the breeze under my skirt, tickling my thighs.

Now I can feel the tickling of my thighs again, only now it's not the wind.

I can see one of the boy's dark face over me. Where did my underwear go? I wriggle and I can feel them slipping from my knees to my ankles. What day of the week is it? I would know if I could see my underwear. They tell me the day of the week. I'm smart so I can read them, even though they have fancy swirly writing. Mommy says it's called cursive. I just know that it's pretty and my panties make me feel pretty. I was stealing them from stores for a while but store clerks kept catching me so now I've stopped. That was after that bad visit with Daddy and Trudi. Now I have new underwear and now I can smile more for Mommy.

The tickling is changing. The tingling is familiar but I can't figure out why.

I'm back in the room now, but I'm not sure how to stay on the table. It feels more like wrestling, but I feel all tingly down there. The boys are taking turns being over me. I'm trying to be polite but I don't know what I'm supposed to say. I want them to like me and I don't want anything to happen to my dress. I go limp.

I start seeing everything from up above, like I'm a spider up high on the wall, tucked up against the ceiling. I can see them, I can see me, but I'm not me. It's like watching television only I'm the star. A dark star.

Voices, adult voices, are coming closer to the shed. The boys scurry like roaches to the door and leave all at once. I jump down off the table and pull my silky panties up. I feel numb, mostly on the inside, so it takes me a minute to leave the shed.

It seems so much brighter outside than when we came in. My eyes are watering at the light; it must be the light. I look down at my shoes and make sure they still look shiny like they did when Mommy dropped me off this morning. She should be here any minute.

I find myself on a swing, getting my happy face together. I can't tell Mommy about the shed. She might get upset. She probably knows I shouldn't be in there. Bad girls sneak off. She needs me to be a good girl. A good girl with wispy blonde hair and soulful blue eyes and a cute, chubby smile.

"Bridget, your mom is here."

Off I waddle, straightening my dress and hair, hopeful I won't fail her. I remember a time I failed her so terribly. I did my best but my best wasn't good enough. I cried. Crying doesn't work; it just makes things worse. So much worse. There won't be any tears today. Not this time.

~

Reseda, California
1972, Age 1

It's so dark in here.

And still so loud. My breathing is so fast. I feel like I'm suffocating. I have to be quiet. He might hear me in here and hurt me again. My head is pounding and spinning at the same time.

I don't understand what's happening. My head hurts. My whole body hurts. My face stings. I can feel wetness streaming down my face.

Is it my tears? No, it's coming from my forehead. It's on my hands. I taste it and it's not watery. It's thick.

I saw him hitting Mommy, taking her by the ponytail and swinging her around the room.

She laughed at him.

You never laugh at Daddy. He doesn't like that.

He calls her bad names and hits her. I cry when he does that, and then he turns to me. He hates it when I cry. I can see it in his eyes; the hate, the rage. I'm in my crib; I can't escape. He's coming for me.

He gives me something to really cry about. It hurts. I fall back against the rails. I cry harder. I want to stop crying but I can't. It hurts and I'm scared. Mommy comes toward me but he hits her again, she slams into the crib. She reaches for me.

I'm on the ground, out of the crib. Something splatters on me. It joins the stuff that's already streaming down my head. I scramble for the door.

I have to find a place to hide. I wish I could walk better. I'm just learning and I wobble a lot. I crawl faster and so I let myself fall and crawl.

I find a closet. It's open a crack so I can get in there. I try to shut the door, stretching for the knob. I flop down onto the clothes piled under me. The pretty dress I wore for my first birthday is still in the dirty laundry. I love that dress. It made me so happy. I got so much cake and frosting on it. I wonder if I sucked on it if it would taste as sweet? I miss sweet.

I feel socks.

Socks make me remember my kitty, Socks. Socks was cute. Socks jumped on things a lot. She jumped on my high chair to visit me. Daddy didn't like it when she jumped on my high chair to visit me. He yelled at her and she didn't listen.

Socks needed to listen.

Daddy grabbed my kitty and took her off my highchair and away from me, out of the kitchen. Mommy ran away toward Daddy and my kitty. She screamed, "no, Jerry!"

Daddy's voice was angry, like it is today. I heard a loud bang. Daddy stormed into the kitchen. Socks didn't come back.

Socks doesn't jump on my highchair anymore.

I miss my kitty. No more thinking about my kitty because thinking about her makes me sad. If I get sad I'll cry and make noise and I won't be hidden anymore.

I feel like I've been here forever. I want to come out but I can't. It's worse out there. Mommy's screaming. I hate it when she screams.

Bad things happen when she's loud, just like when I'm loud.

Sometimes when he's loud it's okay, but that's when it's loud happy. This isn't loud happy. I know loud happy. I giggle sometimes and that loud is okay, too. My giggle makes things better.

Today is the bad loud.

There's a banging at the door. Not the closet door but a faraway door. I think it's the door to the outside. Things get quiet fast. I hear voices. Men's voices. Then footsteps. They are searching. For what? I hear Mommy calling to me. I don't want to answer.

Quiet is better.

But my head hurts and I'm all wet and drippy and I'm thirsty. But I stay quiet. Quiet is safe. The closet is safe.

The closet door opens and the light rushes in. It makes me squint hard and put my head down. It's quiet. I slowly look up. Men I don't know tower over me. The men wear uniforms.

They look so sad.

I want to smile to make their sad stop but I can't. I lost my smiles. One of the men squats down to look at me. Now his face is close to mine.

His sad gets bigger.

I catch it. I start to cry, but quiet crying. He wipes my face and now his hand is red and drippy. I am messy. I don't like being messy.

I look around and I see lots of red. I don't like red. He gets up and Mommy's face is close now and hers is all red and drippy, too.

I hate red, drippy faces.

I see the men in blue talking with Daddy. They leave with him. I hear one say, "it'll give you time to cool down."

Cool sounds good because cool makes me think of blue and I like blue. Blue is the color of sky and I like sky.

Nothing pretty is red. Not here. Blue is better.

Our towels are blue. Mommy wipes us both with the blue towel. The drippy stops. I get my sippy cup with water so the thirsty can stop.

I like stops.

I lay down with Mommy, looking out the window to the blue sky and I feel nothing.

Nothing is better than something today.

~

Amherst, Massachusetts
1989, Age 18

In less than a minute, I regret my decision to get in this elevator. Trapped in a four-by-four-foot box offers no relief. Thankfully, it gives me my freedom back at the push of a button.

I race to my room, head down, as though a blizzard surrounds me.

The familiar rush fills my consciousness. Drowning in emotion again, I see no shore. I want this feeling to be gone. Death beckons me once again. What can I take? I can't stand blood so I must overdose. Where can I get drugs? Coming up empty, I recall stories about students jumping off one of the 20-plus story buildings that ensconce me. That would hurt. And be traumatizing for onlookers. I can't do that; leave the world like that. Tears well up in my eyes as I realize that the only person who can commit my suicide is me, and the only person who can decide to live is me.

I pick up the clunky room phone with the big buttons and call the number I've resisted calling so many times before, unwilling to admit my weakness. There's no avoiding the truth:

I'm out of control.

A woman's voice greets me on the other end, "Crisis line, this is Amanda. How are you?"

Her gentle voice reminds me of another woman who had taken my call three years before when I was still in high school and could see no other option then to end it all. Back then it was the Good Samaritans and my friend, Donna, had dialed the phone for me.

Like reciting facts for an exam, I share the high points of my abuse history with the volunteer on the other end of the phone. I'm not really interested in offering up my vulnerability to a total stranger, yet I had few defenses at this point. Bursting into tears stored for far too many years, I unload my story onto this poor, unsuspecting soul. The abuse, abandonment, loss, self-hatred, and disorders come tumbling out of my mouth, seeking air like a fish seeks water.

I rattle off the high points of my history all to explain why tonight I want to die. Again. Why I can't go on like this. How crazy I feel. How overwhelming every minute of every day has become. I don't want to fight anymore. Exhaustion overcomes me. All the time. She listens so sincerely, sighing and gasping at the right intervals, showing me she hears me with her ears and her heart.

Before we hang up the phone, she demands that I hold myself to a safety plan we constructed. You know, that I'd call or speak to someone about my plan to end my life before I actually tried it. She sets up a meeting with a counselor at the center later that week, gaining my commitment that I wouldn't try to kill myself before calling the number again. Luckily, my lack of impulse control is mediated by my lack of access to drugs to overdose on and my unwillingness to splatter like a watermelon on the pavement.

~

Sitting with the counseling center's therapist fills me with panic. She means well but the look of horror on her face as I share my history tells me that I am too much for her to handle. I can't trust my story and my pain with just anyone. I require fierce. Courageous. She seems neither.

I move on.

The following morning, I call another local therapist, to take control over my grief, my trauma. To wrestle down the ghosts that haunt every waking hour. To set my frantic mind at ease.

Two days later, I make my way over to Northampton, a quaint, progressive town that borders Amherst to the west. I don't feel nearly cool enough to pull my vanilla sedan through this bastion of progressive ideals and eclectic shops and dining establishments.

Months later, I'll find myself two streets over, listening to the musician who sang the lyrics of my pain, Melissa Etheridge, in the intimate concert hall at Smith College.

Today, I focus on garnering the courage to walk into a stranger's office and reveal my deepest, darkest secrets. Allow her to see my fragile rawness, my unadulterated shame, my boundless misery. To admit to another human being that I'm broken, damaged, and hopelessly flawed, deserving of the abuse peppering my existence since birth. Unless her name is "Dr. Miracle Worker," failure seems imminent.

I pull into a spot on the backside of a nondescript house on the edge of town, flanked by parking spots and unruly bushes desperate for a trimming. I make my way up the rickety wooden stairs on the backside of the house, my heart thumping out of my chest with every step.

What will she think of me? What will she do with me?

I need to seem somewhat together or she might have the men in white coats show up and I'll end up in a looney bin, blowing my semester and forever marking myself as a crazy person. Anything but that.

Hold it together, Bridget. Hold it together. Show her how you are managing, you just need some pointers on how to manage better. You got this.

I enter what appears to be a waiting room with a perfectly appointed sofa, matching cushioned chairs and a coffee table adorned with fresh magazines. I quickly sit down on the edge of the sofa, conscious of taking up the least amount of space possible. Nothing worse than a fat, broken, ugly girl.

I think of the list I made in my journal; a list of songs I want played at my funeral. "Amazing Grace" and "The Angels" by Melissa Etheridge are among the chosen ballads. If people couldn't grasp my agony as I walked among them, maybe they'll finally understand after I'm gone.

My thoughts return to this room, reluctantly. The waiting is filling me with a darkness I can't name.

Just when I think I'm going to suffocate under the weight of my grief and embarrassment, a tall, lean woman with a pixie haircut dressed in a loose-fitting sweater, khakis, and hippie sandals emerges from what must be the office. She greets me and all I want to do is shrink into the nearest hole in the wall and disappear. She seems to take note of my discomfort and motions for me to join her in her office. I sense her pity and disdain for me, seeing right through my ridiculous outer shell.

I was a fool to think she wouldn't immediately assess me for what I am: A pathetic disaster. I'm annoying her already and I haven't even been here two minutes. I want to run. But I sit.

"What brings you here today, Bridget?"

Oh, where to start? I'm eighteen years old and I feel 90. I'm crawling on the ground, dragging my tired, aching spirit to the threshold. I haven't a clue on where to begin.

I simply start.

I let the story unfold as she takes copious notes, looking up intermittently to meet my gaze. I reach for numbness but grab hold of excruciating pain instead. I want to stop but I know that won't make anything any better. Oh, sweet relief find me.

If it was physically possible, I would become one with the cushy sofa I'm seated in. I sink further and further into it as she asks me probing questions about each experience, like scraping an acid-soaked knife into the open wounds I've never managed to heal on my own.

We spend nearly two hours together and we've only covered a portion of my history. I want to press on and get it over with. I need relief, damn it. She reacts to my shifting body language, pausing to gather her words.

I'm sure she's going to tell me that she can't help me; that I'm hopeless.

Instead, she reaches for her calendar and schedules our next visit, this time up the road from my college in nearby Amherst.

She sees my brokenness and warns me how hard purging my demons is going to be. She recognizes how lucky I am to still be alive, to have survived to this point.

Catching my breath, I breathe a sigh of relief. I might just live through this after all.

~

Dearest Bridget,

You don't know how close you are to salvation.

If you reached out you could literally touch it with your fingertips, brushing its soft, warm, fullness. I'm not going to bullshit you, though. The road out is a dark and winding one. You have formed ideas about yourself and the world in ways that don't serve you. Understandable and necessary, they rob you of joy, peace, and love.

That just won't do.

You've got to deconstruct, piece by piece, each of your perceptions and the feelings and responses that sprung from them. Some parts will take longer than others. Your mission then was to survive. Your call now is to thrive. You've already survived. You've made it this far, collecting bumps and bruises along the way.

The only way out is through.

You're going to collect coins from countless 12-Step meetings. You know you're broken yet you don't know where to find the healing. What's the injury that needs the most attention? Is it the sexual abuse you endured? Could it be your eating disorders? Perhaps it was growing up with addicts? Maybe you're an addict yourself? Do you need to find religion? Which God fits? Like Homer's Odyssey, you launch your quest to find the promise land. A welcome shore. To experience a day free of angst. Just one day. To find the answers to the questions that plague you. So many questions that spring eternal from just one:

Why?

In the years to come, you'll answer that question so many ways, to differing depths with varying shades of relief. There are no easy responses, trust me. Explanations are elusive, but there is healing that comes from drawing them into the light.

Your courage to fight your demons will inspire others in myriad ways. They'll draw on your strength to chase their own recovery. Many will embrace newly-found gratitude for having dodged the many bullets you've absorbed. You'll inspire them to face things that haven't even happened to them yet, knowing that if you could, they can. Your wry, self-effacing wit brings levity to the most disturbing conversations.

You mention what you had for dinner the night before with similar emotion to describing being beaten as a baby by your own father.

It's unsettling, to say the very least.

Do less of that. You'll alienate people and you won't understand why. Given your past, you'll see their departures as confirmation of your badness. It's not that simple. It's just too damn much for some people to digest. You've been through some serious shit and most people can't relate to that level of soul evisceration. Your job is not to tip toe around others, just to take their feelings into account while you process your own.

You're more than your abusive history, so lead with other magnificent pieces of you whenever possible.

This advice will fall on deaf ears, I know, since all you can see right now is your pain and the scars it left behind. In this developmental stage, you really believe that you and the abuse are one and the same. It's okay. This will pass. You'll find ways to acknowledge its pivotal role in your life yet see how much more there is to you, if only to see the good you've done with the bad.

Fewer people over time will know you as "Bridget who has endured so much" than know you as "Bridget who has accomplished so much."

Later still, the world will know you as "Bridget who endured so much has accomplished so much." Someday, you will be integrated.

Why?

As I keep telling you and you are starting to feel, you are powerful. You are meant to do great things, to feel great love, and to share great healing. You are not defined by your past. You are defined by wrestling it down to the ground, ripping out the beauty, and burning down the pain to form a beacon of unending love, compassion, and forgiveness.

You, my dearest Bridget, are a loving warrior of life. Welcome to the doorway to the other side of your journey.

~ Love, Me

~ Epilogue ~

By the time I got to college, my own addictions and relationships were reaching a breaking point. I'd rushed into a romantic relationship right out of high school, getting engaged just a few months in. We set a date for the month after I turned 18, moving together to Florida after my first semester in college as we planned our wedding. I broke it off and moved back to Massachusetts two months before the wedding. Talk about high drama.

I sank into a depression, gaining weight, cutting off my long hair, and finding myself struggling with significant health issues. I'm nothing if not famous for psychosomatic occurrences! When I returned back to school for my second year of college, I was a hot, broken mess. The story I started with at the beginning of this chapter occurred at the end of that first semester back at school. Breaking point...rock bottom...crossroads...take your pick. I had reached mine and it hurt like hell.

I felt fat, dirty, lonely, unloved, and broken. I was looking for salvation and couldn't find even a flashlight to illuminate the way. I'd left my fiancé. I had cleared my proverbial slate (no boyfriend, living away from my parents, sister was incarcerated). I was free, untethered physically and felt lost. I was exploding and imploding at the same time. I knew I needed to transform but I had no clue as to how to do that. I was suffocating under the weight of my shame and self-loathing. I was promiscuous, just trying to numb out the tidal wave of feelings that overwhelmed me. This behavior just made things worse, even in the moment. I hung inspirational posters, cartoons, and sayings on the wall in my dorm room to inspire me. I can't say that I was inspired, but they got me to put one foot in front of the other most days so I could simply endure.

By the time I found myself in that elevator, I had tried everything I knew to move through the perpetual crisis I felt myself ensnared in. I wanted to live another way but I had no flipping clue how to make that happen. I would find myself at a series of 12-step meetings over the subsequent year which would give me a way to frame this state of mind: I needed to surrender to something stronger than myself because my ways just weren't cutting it. I stumbled into religious cult meetings searching for light, peace, and safety. In my vulnerable state, I was blessed to recognize them for what they were quickly enough to avoid their dangers.

I had seen many therapists before the one I finally opened up to in that little office in Northampton, but I wasn't interested in telling them my stuff. I hid. Or I blurted it all out but had no hope that anyone would listen or do anything. No one ever had. They were powerless or uninterested. They just made me feel more alone. More crazy. More damaged. Not worth saving.

My recovery was anchored in my therapist's office and in a book that literally saved my life by giving me the validation and understanding I craved: "Courage to Heal." It told me that I wasn't alone, that my experiences were shared with others who had to crawl out of those dark, ugly places.

The sexual abuse that peppered my childhood memories drove me to madness, depression, and suicide attempts. That book gave me a talisman to grieve it, understand myself, and feel like I wasn't alone in all of the crazy thoughts, feelings, and behaviors I contended with.

Thankfully, in my therapist I found a guide to walk with me down that long and winding path I call "recovery." It was the first step in a long journey to reclaim my life force, my joy, my potential. I am forever grateful.

Before I rose up from my little landslides, I set up camp on the rocky ground, becoming blistered and bruised at the hands of those I was told to trust and love. From the very beginning, I was conditioned to suffering and sought it out like manna from Heaven.

"More than anything
I wanted to heal you
To dip my hand into the icy, raging river of your pain
And draw out polished stones one by one." ~ K. Augustus

CHAPTER TWO
BROKEN

力

Mission Hills, California
1973, Age 2

The red is back.

The hard, cool floor underneath me trembles as Daddy thunders toward Mommy. My block tower falls over. It was so pretty and tall. I want to build it again but I'm stuck. I'm a statue. I want to move but I can't. I get so calm I can't hear my breathing anymore. I wonder if I can be quiet enough to disappear? I've never been that quiet.

It's not quiet now. It's loud. It's like watching my favorite show, Romper Room, on the television. I wonder if it's on right now? I don't want to move in case they don't notice me sitting there. "Who do I see? I can see Mommy and Daddy..."

It started in the kitchen like it always does.

I know this because I study them. Everyday. All day long. Are they loud? Is there silence? How do Daddy's footsteps sound?

Is there happy or is there sad? Are they playing with me or are they only talking to each other? It's better when I'm in the middle. I do lots of things to bring the smiles to their faces. They take pictures of me. I dance for them sometimes because I'm a good dancer. Sometimes they dance. I watch. Are they dancing together or is Mommy dancing for Daddy?

Some nights, they speak of how they met. How Daddy saw Mommy on stage and thought she was beautiful. She danced for him and he gave her money because she did such a good job. Mommy is a good dancer. Daddy stares at her when she dances. And smiles. After the staring, he picks her up and takes her into the bedroom. I think she dances more for him in there because he's usually smiling when they return. They go in there a lot. Daddy doesn't work so whenever Mommy is home he is right up against her.

I am a good girl. I stay quiet. I play on my own. I practice my happy. Sometimes they put me in my jumping seat in the doorway. I could bounce for hours and hours. Up and down and up and down and up and down. Sometimes I'm bouncy on Daddy's lap. I'm good at bouncing up and down.

I'm not good at anything today. I didn't see this storm coming so I'm in the way. Daddy screams at Mommy, "I told you never to laugh at me. You remember what happened the last time you laughed at me?"

I do. I remember. I watched. She laughed at him. His fist came down like a flash of light right into her belly. She dropped to her knees. He grabbed her by the hair flipped her around. Her face was in the carpet. The carpet is better than the tile. You can see the red on the tile. The carpet hides the red. Mommy screamed a lot. She begged him to stop. He never listens to begging. He had her bent over like a dog on the ground. She wailed as he banged up against her over and over. "You want to be an ass? You'll get it in the ass like the bitch that you are!" He kept banging at her until he got tired, I guess. She slumped to the floor and cried.

He turned to me next.

It's happening again today.

I know what's coming. I hate what's coming. I can see it in his eyes. I try to make my sad go away so he won't have his mad get bigger but my sad is so big. He can see it and it's just like when Mommy laughs at him. His freckled face gets so red, so tight. His fists clench. I don't bother running away. He always catches me when I try. He's so big, so strong. I am not. I am weak. I am bad. Bad girls get hurt.

Now I hurt. My insides and my outsides hurt. Everything is moving all at once. I know something is mixing with my insides, but my face is on the carpet and I can't see what's happening. I can't feel where he ends and I begin.

I don't bother crying. Crying never helps.

It'll be over soon. It always is. Then we'll clean up the red. It's easier when I go potty to clean up the red. I'm a good girl because I go on the potty now. I make Mommy happy when I sit on the potty and let everything come out there instead of in my diaper. I just sit and let it come out till it stops.

There's a picture on the wall I stare at while I wait. It shows a naked man standing in a stream with lots of trees around him. The sun shines in to light up the stream. It's so calm.

I want to be wherever that is. So I go there. I feel the cool water on my toes, the damp, fresh air surrounding me. The frogs splashing over my feet, the tiny fish swimming between my ankles. There are no voices. No crying. No yelling. No bleeding. No pain. Just birds chirping from up above. I am soothed.

I am anywhere but here.

I am nowhere.

~

Oh, Sweet Jesus.

How did you not break forever that fateful day? And all the days after and before it that looked the same? No one should be violated that way, their body used to satisfy a hunger for demeaning, sexual domination. And by your own father? What sense could you make of that, him touching you the way you watched him touch your mother? His pain and rage overflowing, he almost killed you with it. Over and over and over again. In the spaces between, he cuddled and played with you. You lived in the extremes.

You are just a baby, not even two years old, and you already can't distinguish between love and abuse. They are one and the same. This will fuck you up good as you get older. You will find yourself in abusive relationships time after time, thirsting to find love from those who just want to use you. Dominate you. Merge with you. You will acquiesce to their demands, wanting to please them so they won't reject you. So that they won't leave you. When men touch you in the future, you'll leave that body of yours and witness what's happening from far away. You'll be safe there, don't worry. It'll be like watching a movie. I know you'll give yourself away more than you really want to, and you'll make it all about them, their pleasure. You are so afraid of your own. You guard it like a talisman. That's okay. I understand.

You'll also find lovers who will want to love this whole experience right out of you. Like the first one who noticed the long, thick, raised scar from the edge of your rectum upward, showing where your father literally tore you in two. Your lover will be patient and kind, wanting you to release that pain to the wind. He will love you so much that there will be moments when you're back in your body for a time.

You are more than your broken body, my dear girl. You are more than the pain you endure and the pleasure you offer.

You are so much more than that.

You will find people, angels really, along your journey who will remind you of your value. They will see the light inside of you that has been dimmed by those people who lived in their own consuming darkness. You will get sucked in, and then you will crawl your way out, grabbing for any stable piece of dirt you can find.

You are a survivor, a thriver, and you will not be crushed by this. This will define you only as much as you let it.

You are powerful. More powerful than anyone who has ever or will ever hurt you. You're a fucking Amazonian warrior of love and light. Sick bastards may seek to destroy you in their own melodrama, but you will not be destroyed. You will bear the scars, but you will not be the wound.

Do you know what I love most about you?

You could be filled with rage and turn that onto others like they have done unto you. Or you could do the same to random people in your path. But you don't. You choose love over hate. More often than not, you use the rage buried deep inside of you to fuel your hunger to know love, to feel peace. You rage against the storm which is your God-given right. You have seen Hell and you have the burns to prove it. Over time, you will find people you can trust to heal you, piece by piece.

Piece by piece, you'll be whole again.

~ Love, Me

CHAPTER THREE
TRASH

Cool, California
1975, Age 3

I can't believe I'm really here! I'm finally with Daddy! I haven't seen him in so long! The last time I saw him I wasn't even three fingers old. Now I'm three fingers and a half a finger old. I'm getting to be a big girl. So I got to fly on the plane all by myself! There was a pretty lady who worked on the plane who talked with me a lot while we flew. She made me feel special and made sure I got to Daddy when we landed.

It's the first morning of my visit and Daddy promised that he and Trudi would make pancakes. I love pancakes so much. Mommy puts lots of things inside my pancakes cuz she knows that I'll eat it if it's in a pancake. Pancakes are so yummy.

As I make my way to the table, I ask Daddy if he likes my nightgallon with all the pretty flowers on it. He tells me it's called a nightgown but I tell him that's not what I call it. He smiles. I like it when he smiles. It makes my insides warm and that feels good.

The kitchen table is the shape of paper money, with hard chairs. I need a phone book to sit on to see over the table but he doesn't have one of those so I can hardly see my pancakes. They are stacked so high with lots of syrup. These are going to be messy, I just know it.

They are buttery and so good. They are thicker than Mommy's. I asked for two cuz that's how many I eat at Mommy's. I can't finish two of these. Each one covers almost the whole plate. I'm trying so hard to finish them cuz Daddy doesn't like it when I don't finish my food.

But I just can't. I'm getting slower and slower, and Daddy notices from the kitchen. The light from outside shines in the kitchen window which makes me squint. As he moves quickly toward me I can see him better. His face is all red with scary wrinkles. I know what this means. The mad is coming. No. The mad is already here.

He's so big.

Big like my pancakes only so much bigger. I think his head hits the ceiling.

Not now. Now, his head is in my face, pointing his finger at me. He's angry I'm not eating my pancakes anymore. He's mad that Trudi worked so hard and I'm not being polite. I want to be polite to his girlfriend. I'm just not hungry anymore. He's getting louder and his face is getting redder.

I hate red. I'm shivering but I'm not cold. I can't move. There's no room between Daddy and me and the chair is pressing hard against my back. Maybe that's me doing the pressing.

Then it happens.

I get warmer. But only between my legs and under my bottom. And wet. So wet.

Oh, no.

I had an accident.

I know better. I know to go on the potty. I've been going on the potty for a long time. I don't know what happened. How could I do this? How could I mess this all up so badly?

He smells it. Or sees it. I can't tell how he figures it out, but he does. His mad gets so big I think it's going to fill the whole house.

Suddenly, Trudi is behind Daddy. He's yelling at her to get something.

He presses his huge hands into my ribs and picks me up and puts me on the floor. Hard.

Trudi comes over with a cup. I drank my milk. Maybe if I drink more milk I won't be in trouble for not eating my pancakes? I hope so. I hate being bad.

She doesn't hand me the cup, though. The cup is empty. Not for long. She's tipping the chair forward, like it tips sometimes when I get off of it. There's a lot of pee on my chair and now all that pee is in the cup. Daddy tells me to get back on the chair. I'm wetter than the chair so I guess it doesn't matter.

"Drink this!" Daddy is yelling as he slams the cup onto the table in front of me. I know it's my pee and I know that's not what I drink but I can't tell Daddy "no" now. Not ever. I'm shivering again. I know what I have to do but I don't want to. It's warm. I like cold drinks. It smells yucky. I know when things smell yucky they taste even yuckier.

"Drink it!" I don't think his mad can get any bigger than this. I'd better drink this fast before I see more of the red I've seen before. Trudi isn't saying anything. She stepped back into the kitchen after she poured it in the cup for me. She's little and Daddy is so big. Maybe she doesn't like the red either.

I drink it. I do it fast cuz fast is better. There is no good here, but better is still better.

"That's the last time you'll pull a stunt like that!"

Daddy seems better, too, so I leave the table to change my clothes. When I get back, Daddy has a big paper bag in his hands. It's full of smelly trash from the kitchen.

Outside the trailer, on the far side of the dusty lot, stands a wire mesh compost bin as tall as Daddy. I don't understand compost, I just know that rotting food goes in there. The only open space is as high as Daddy's shoulders. The rest of it is filled with smelly trash.

Daddy says "the punishment should fit the crime. This will teach you."

He leads me out to the compost bin. He says I need to put each piece of waste from the bag into the bin. My tiny fingers squeeze into the trash, sinking into partially decomposed food. There are those white worms. I think they are called maggots. They squirm between my fingers as I push another eggshell into it. I want to stop but Daddy is sitting on the steps smoking a cigarette, watching me.

"Finished."

I really am.

~

Oh, Bridget,

This is madness.

You're so little, so fragile, so gentle, yet the world keeps treating you like a criminal. Beating you into submission, shaming you into the corner of your own world. It's wrong. It's inexcusable. Yet it's happening. It keeps happening.

Just when you think it'll stop, it doesn't.

You looked forward to this visit for months and months. You pulled together all of your 3-year-old courage to get on that giant airplane all by yourself and fly there and back. You did it because missed your daddy, even though doing so makes so little sense.

He's stripped you of your innocence and layers of your humanity, yet he's showered you with love and affection.

He sent you home with nightmares and stuffed animals.

You want one to the exception of the other but you don't wield that power. He holds all the power now. He and your mother. Neither one of them seem interested in your well-being, especially if it conflicts with their own selfish needs. That's not how it's supposed to be, but you haven't a clue about that. What you know to be truth is the truth.

It won't always be this way.

As hard as it is to say, you'll be grateful for the postcard your daddy sent to you after this visit, apologizing for what happened, even though he doesn't give your experience any specificity. It's okay; you know what happened.

You'll never forget what happened.

You'll tell it to yourself over and over again to keep it real because you're the only one who will. I'm so sorry for that. I'm sorry that it happened to you in the first place, and I'm sorry that it'll haunt you. You'll feverishly try to make sense of it. How could someone who loves you do that to you? How could he have that much anger toward you? Is that what you deserve? How will anyone love you the way you want to be loved if this is how you understand love? Is this as good as it gets?

It's not. These were his demons coming to the surface. He isn't good at being a daddy. Even though he can see how precious and amazing you are, he doesn't have the capacity to treat you how you deserve to be treated. That's sad. Sad for him and sadder still for you.

No one deserves to be hurt like this. He scared you; you peed yourself. He literally scared the piss out of you. That's so natural, Sweetie. Not only just because it is, but because he's damaged you so badly in the past that your body reacts to his fury with the only defenses it has. If fault is to be assigned, it is his. That trash nonsense was reprehensible. He did it to shame and terrify you; like you needed any more of that? You absolutely did not. You needed comfort, apology, and love. You needed to have your broken little shell understood, accepted. This was violation on top of violation.

38

When will it end?

I wish I could tell you that this is the end of it. In some ways it is. He won't ever hurt you physically again. Emotionally, psychologically: He's just getting started.

The pain he heaves on you won't end until he's dead to the world, or at least dead to you. In the meantime, nibble on the idea that his actions aren't a reflection of your value; never have been, never will be. Whatever he says or doesn't say, does or doesn't do: That's his story, not yours. You are and will be loved more deeply than you think possible right now.

For now, and for always, don't swallow the poison he offers. Save yourself, my love. Save yourself. Years from now, when your father murders Trudi, the silent one, you'll realize something.

You are the lucky one.

~ Love, Me

BACKSTORY ONE
HOTEL
CALIFORNIA

力

"We already live on the planet of war,
we already live on the red planet,
and it's a war against children.
All the other wars are just the shadows
of the war on children." ~ Stefan Molyneux

~

My father raped me. My mother knew.

My father raped my mother. I knew.

Unlike those gut-wrenching stories of school-age children having their bedrooms visited by their molester, I was first violated by my abuser before I had conscious memory. How do I know that it happened? I know because my mother saw fit to share these traumatic details with me for as long as I can remember. How my father became enraged if she laughed at him. When she crossed him like that, her payment was being raped, usually anally. How he beat her, beat me, left her without some of her teeth.

He started beating me when I was eight weeks old. Eight WEEKS old. I was too young to resist, to get away. I shared a couple of vignettes of the abuse I was born into; there was so much more. It was a way of life. Though, once would have been enough to leave indelible marks on anyone's spirit.

The damage that the violence did was outdone only by her telling me how much she continued to love him, even years later after their divorce and our move to Massachusetts, 3,000 miles away. How she pined for him, crying herself to sleep some nights hoping for his return. How she calmed her longing by relying on his promise that they would grow old together, requiring her promise to never marry another man.

He almost killed us. Yet, no one could love us more than him. We suffered unspeakable brutality at his hands. Yet, we could love no one more than him.

Even worse than that epic brain twist, my mom said that I chose my life, my parents, my abuse. She said that I *wanted* this experience. That all of this was done with my soul's permission and direction. That pained me more than anything. I couldn't even grieve the mistreatment because I'd done it to myself. I was masochistic yet writhing in a sea of misery that I picked out on the buffet line of soul selection. Talk about pathetic.

There is a photo in a frame that has adorned my house since I was little. Now it's on the cover of this book. It's a photo of me, barely two, standing next to my father who is on one knee. And a lion. Yes, that's a *real* lion. We are on the rickety porch of an old shack. The lion is laying down in front of me, his massive countenance larger than three of me. It's a disturbing image, yet deeply symbolic of the power and terror, danger and beauty, fear and courage that defined my young life.

I was very good at being invisible, at least in pockets. I was stealing underwear from stores at age three and I could never fully comprehend why my mother didn't do anything to get me help. She knew about my thievery since the store management brought her to task right along with me. She told me years later that she suspected why I was stealing underwear but didn't know how to help. So she didn't. She told me the stories of our shared abuse over and over again but still spoke of the timeless love she shared with my dad.

Why?

To understand why people do what they do it helps to understand them. People are complicated, far more so than we often contemplate. And so it was with my parents.

My father was twenty when he married my mother. She was five years older than him, with a marriage and a child under her belt. She was working as a stripper (a.k.a., exotic dancer) when he came to the club, staying until her shift was over so he could take her out to breakfast.

How romantic.

He came from a fatherless home, his dad leaving his mom and two older siblings before he was born. He blamed himself at some level for his father's abandonment and his mother did nothing to ease that burden. To say he had parenting deficits is a clear understatement. Growing up in Kansas before moving to California, he spent his teens as a delinquent, getting expelled from high school after pushing his teacher out a window.

Yeah, he was *that* guy.

He joined the Army and got his GED during basic training; the same time he got disabled during a bar fight. He suffered injuries that surfaced a blood clotting disorder that, over time, basically robbed him of the use of his legs. He had multiple pulmonary embolisms, heart attacks, and even a stroke before he was 23. His heavy cigarette smoking, drinking, and drug use certainly didn't help his medical condition. He couldn't hold a job and was in and out of the hospital, tolerating a great deal of pain in the interim. By his definition, he wasn't a man.

His wife, my mom, worked to support them, leaving him to care for me while she worked. He was my primary caretaker. The stay-at-home parent. With undisturbed access to me.

His woman, my mother, was feisty. She was a single mom when they met, recently divorced from an older, alcoholic man. During my parents' courtship, my mother lost custody of her first daughter (my half-sister). Working as a stripper, living with an unemployed, younger man, who both self-medicated their manic depression with drugs and alcohol, her parents testified against her citing her as an unfit parent.

Years later, she would play out this Freudian drama with me, only this time it was done without merit since my life was calm and without addiction, lawlessness, and mental health issues and my ex-husband's abuse was well known. She spurred me to leave him and helped me each step along the journey, then turned on me and almost succeeded in having my children taken away from me. If it wasn't for the moment that she revealed her batshit crazy self to opposing counsel, she might have actually carried it out. I'm not sure what this would have healed in her damaged psyche, if anything, but I'm blessed I never had to find out. Thanks, Mom.

Unrestrained, my mother's penchant for drama was downright dangerous, then and always.

Isolated from family, my parents' addictions, vices, and violence spun out of control.

Then came Bridget.

My father demanded my conception; my mother resisted given her despair over losing custody of her first-born who celebrated her fifth and sixth birthdays away from our mom. See, with the tacit support of my mom's parents, my half-sister's father fled the state with her, for years, beyond my conception and birth.

Strangely enough, I almost wasn't born at all. The famous San Fernando (also known as the Sylmar) earthquake occurred on the morning of February 9, 1971 which caused the structural collapse of several medical facilities in the area (and over 1,000 landslides in the region). My mother had a pre-natal appointment that morning, just a couple of hours after the earthquake, in one of the buildings that collapsed. Over 2,000 people were injured and 64 people died that morning. Had the earthquake held off for 90 minutes, my mother and I would have likely perished. My luck began before I took my first breath.

After I was born, my half-sister visited briefly and sporadically with us while we lived in California. Some of those visits were pleasant, some not so much. My parents were ill-equipped to be parents and they struggled, a struggle made worse through their rampant drug and alcohol use and frequent partying. My father helped to make ends meet by dealing, and sometimes manufacturing, illegal drugs.

My mother never wanted to be a mother. Not the first time and definitely not the second time. Even with her grandchildren, she was distant and unaffectionate until they were at a conversational age and could meet her need for attention. She bore children because it was what society, and her husbands, expected her to do. She had no interest in it and it showed. She loved us, but her focus was on whoever was in her bed and the drama that her addiction-laden partners surely provided. She loved a good show and reveled in her starring role. Her father was a dynamic, controlling, recovering alcoholic, her mother an emotionally-withholding, overshadowed, co-dependent. Being the youngest by far in her family, she was used to doing whatever necessary to attract attention. To call her a "drama queen" was like calling the Pope "Catholic." In her young adulthood, this meant being in dysfunctional, abusive relationships with men.

Relationships she shared with her innocent offspring.

~

When my mom finally made the decision to break free of my father, she did so by setting him up to get arrested and go to jail. They had a party at our house and my mom tipped off the cops ahead of time. The police arrived during the party and took him to jail but left her to take care of me. She filed for divorce while he awaited trial, driving him straight into the arms of the last mistress he had: Trudi.

My father and Trudi moved to Cool, California, a small, unincorporated community a plane flight north of our house in Los Angeles. The visit with the pancakes and trash marked the first time I'd seen him in many months. And it was the last time I would ever visit with him alone.

I left Los Angeles cheerful and affectionate. I returned withdrawn and moody. I left with a suitcase, I returned with that and three giant stuffed animals Daddy had won for me at the nearby fair.

I left with hope, I returned with none.

Five years would pass before I would lay eyes on him again. I would never see Trudi again.

He killed her before I could.

"This is for the kids who know that the worst kind of fear isn't the thing that makes you scream, but the one that steals your voice and keeps you silent." ~ Abby Norman

CHAPTER FOUR

TAKEN

Franklin, MA
1976, Age 5

I'm so bored. Mommy is looking for material for another project she'll never finish. She has they laying all over our apartment. They just sit there. I want her to make things for me but she promises and never does what she says she will. This fabric warehouse is endless. I just want to leave but Mommy is lost in the stacks, examining every bolt of fabric they have.

I give up. I'll just walk home. It took us about ten minutes to drive here and I know there was only one turn from where we live so I think I can figure it out. The bell on the door dings behind me but I don't think Mommy even noticed amidst the clamor in the store.

I feel like I've been walking forever but I'm nowhere near home. What if I hitchhiked? Mommy picks up hitchhikers all the time so I know how it works. You walk backwards and stick your thumb out while you smile at the cars. I'll do my best. I really don't want to walk back to the store and I don't know if I can make it all the way home. I want to beat Mommy home.

Look! A car is stopping! A man about Mommy's age stops in a little car like ours. He asks me where I'm going so I tell him. He's not going that far but he tells me he will take me part of the way. Part of the way is better than no way. I get in the front seat next to him. I'm friendly and talkative like the people we pick up. I want to do this right.

When I get out, I take the hitchhiker position right away again on the sidewalk so I don't miss a chance to get another ride. A car pulls over. It's a station wagon so it probably has a family in it. A family would be fun to ride with, even if it's only a short time till they drop me off.

As I get in the middle row I see that there are two older boys in the row with me. They put me in the middle cuz I'm the smallest by a lot. Their mom is driving and asks me where I'm headed. I tell her the cross-street that is right next to our building so she will know when to stop. The riders we get do that ahead of time and it helps Mommy. I want to be helpful.

The car is moving and so are the boys. They are putting their hands all over my body and telling me how they aren't going to let me go. I sit still, like a statue, waiting for the corner I told the Mommy to stop at.

She drives right past it.

I yell to her to stop the car. She laughs and says, "no." We are passing my intersection and going the wrong way. We are headed away from my house. She won't stop. I'm so scared. Will I get out of here? If I do, how will I figure out how to get home? How will I know where I am?

I wriggle and squirm to get away but I can't. I scamper out of my seat and crawl toward the back seat to get away from them. I'm kicking but they are stronger than me. I'm screaming for the mom to stop the car but she's just laughing. I throw myself across the boy on the right and start banging my fists on the window, trying to get people's attention outside the car. The mom is telling the boys to calm me down before I cause a scene. That makes me yell louder and punch harder, clawing at the door handle. The car comes to a screeching halt and I thrust myself out the door onto the curb. I run and I don't stop running until I get home.

When Mommy gets home she finds me on the couch, watching television. I tell her I'm sorry. That's all I tell her. I don't tell Mommy bad things. She has enough bad. She doesn't need my bad, too.

~

Oh, Sweet Child,

Your boldness will be your saving grace and your undoing. You're modeling the behavior you see around you but that's insanity and so friggin dangerous. I'm so proud of you for fighting to get out of that car. That took courage. I know it was inspired by fear, fear of not getting home. You were compliant when the boys were assaulting you, but when you thought you couldn't go home, you fought back. Oh, Bridget. The tracks have been carved in that delicate spirit of yours telling you that you exist for others. You have no idea where you fit in to any of this nonsense going on around you. The blessing is that you have a fighting spirit in your core. Deep down, under all the wreckage, you are powerful. You will rise up in spurts, increasing your endurance for the big fights of your life, later, when you have the ability to do something to protect yourself. These boys were awful; their mother was worse. A mother had a hand in this happening to you. You don't seem surprised, though. Mothers have a way of standing by, blindly, complicitly. You know this all too well.

Years from now you'll be sexually assaulted by a classmate as you wait for the school bus in sixth grade. His friends will help to restrain you and your friend so you can't be rescued. You'll fight back, just like you did today. This time, you'll tell someone about it to make your voice and pain known. The school principal will say the stinging words that so many girls have heard, sending them back into their silent shame:

"Boys will be boys."

Nothing will happen to these boys, either set. The mother will be unscathed, the principal will retire with a pension. You? You'll fight your way to some peace of mind, knowing that although you don't deserve this rocky road, it's the one you must travel.

Walk that road next time. No more rides with strangers. As much as you want to carve your independence from Mommy, first make sure you have a safe place to land. Until you figure out who you can trust, don't give your trust away so easily. Please, Baby, please.

Love, Me

CHAPTER FIVE

TREMORS

East Lexington, MA
1977, Age 6

Mommy is going to be late for work if she doesn't hurry. Our bathroom is connected to my bedroom in the front of the house so I have to pass through it to get to the kitchen. I stop to give her a kiss and hug while she finishes putting on her makeup.

She's so pretty. She would be beautiful without the makeup, but she likes to dress up her eyes and cheeks before she goes to work. I race into the kitchen to find some cereal for breakfast. I'll leave for school after Mommy leaves, but I still don't have much time to spare.

I open the kitchen cabinet and jump back. Roaches. I hate roaches. They scurry so fast you can't catch them but you sure can hear them. We have so many of them that when we open the cabinet for the first time after a few hours, we catch them piled up against the door and they fall to the counter like jellybeans. Only, jellybeans with legs and antennae.

I pour my cereal and add the milk and start to make my way back to my room so I can get dressed. It's probably better to eat in the kitchen but with those nasty bugs crawling around. I want to get as far away from them as possible.

The quiet is broken by a slamming sound coming from the bathroom.

Mommy!

Her reflection in the bathroom mirror scares me. I see in her eyes that she's not there anymore. She's disappeared into herself somehow.

Her eyes are open but they are empty.

Her mouth is open, too, and she's starting to grunt. Her right hand is slamming onto the sink while her left hand tightly grips its edge. I put my cereal down on the toilet seat and wrap my arms around her.

She *has* to feel safe in my arms or she's going to hurt herself.

She lets go of the sink and I pull her down on top of me onto the linoleum floor. I have to keep her head away from the toilet. She's thrashing back and forth like a fish out of water.

I'm forgetting something. She has given me instructions on what to do when her seizures start so I need to remember. She's making gurgling noises now which makes me remember.

Her tongue! I need to make sure that she doesn't choke on her tongue! I shove my hand into her mouth and try to flatten her tongue so it doesn't roll back. I'm holding her body as still as I can so she doesn't hit anything. We are in a small space so there's lots to bang up against. At least I came in when I did.

Mommy has been having these a lot lately. She had one on the train home from Boston last week. I wonder what the people on the train did. Did they look away? Did they stare? Did they hurt her?

I bet no one took care of her like I am now.

She doesn't remember the seizures. She just loses time. Sometimes she loses time without falling on the floor and getting hurt. That faraway look she gets. She just stares into space sometimes and doesn't respond to anyone or anything. I worry she will get lost in her head when she's driving us somewhere.

I need to learn how to steer so I can save us if that happens.

She's told me that a metallic taste fills her mouth right before a seizure happens. I also notice that she scratches her head like she has fleas. I watch for every possible sign. When her gaze wanders. When she loses focus. I craft disaster plans. Answers to "what ifs" fill my brain.

It's the same with her pot. She also calls it marijuana. Her "joints." The ones she smokes in her room, usually later in the evening. She says it helps calm her brain. A calm brain means fewer seizures. Fewer seizures is good. Mommy says it's like bad wiring in her head. Like electricity gone wrong.

I'm scared that her brain will burst or just stop working after it shorts out like that. Would she get electrocuted from the inside out? The pot helps her not short circuit. I have to understand her pot smoking because it's for her health. I get scared sometimes, though. What if the police find out and they arrest her? I would lose my mommy. My daddy wouldn't be helpful. He disappears a lot. They wouldn't let me be with him.

I bought her a pretty stone with a butterfly on it for Mother's Day. I got it at the convenience store up the street. They sell papers and stones and things. They looked at me funny when I asked for the pretty butterfly stone with the holes on either end. "Do you know what this is for?" I nodded. I knew. I know so many, many things. I'm six and I'm really smart. Mommy tells me all the time how smart I am.

~

My dear Bridget,

It's hard to rely on a parent who isn't well. You know this all too well. So many kids out there have a parent or parents who have diseases or disorders and they can totally feel your pain. You live in fear that your mom will be taken away from you, by death or arrest. This is completely natural. It's human and it's smart and it's real. This isn't like the boogeyman. He's not real. This is. So your fears are warranted. You take charge because it makes you feel better, of course, but that's not where the damage of this exists. The real threat is in your upside down thinking that your mother is your responsibility. That you have to save her, fix her, mend her, protect her.

It's not your job. Your job is to be a kid.

You can help, you can. Mostly because you're instinctively a helper. But because it's not your job, that means it's not your fault if she doesn't get well. It's not your fault.

She isn't getting the help she really needs. Instead, she's putting it on you to rescue her from the edge. You're six years old. That just isn't okay.

I know you love feeling grown up and in charge. That's a safe feeling. If you're the boss, you can fix things. If you can fix things, life can get better. If life gets better and you were the cause, you'll feel good about you.

I see the draw, I do. But, I have to tell you the honest truth: This thinking will almost kill you. Not her. You.

If she lets you down — and she will — you'll figure it out. If she kills herself by omission or commission — and she will — you'll be okay. There are angels everywhere, even though you can't always recognize them. They will be present for you and guide you out of every dark place you find yourself.

You'll learn many great lessons from this journey.

You'll learn to take care of yourself and urge others to do the same.

You will seek out the medical community, when it makes sense, and not show up with a "no" before you've thought through a "maybe."

You'll be compassionate for those with medical and mental ailments, but you'll also hold them to the standard of self-care. You'll have little time for the victim-mentality, even your own.

Hold onto those lessons. Remember that you are smart and kind. Loving and generous. Most of all, you are powerful. You will move through this. You will use this experience to make you stronger because that's who you are and what you were meant to do.

~ Love, Me

CHAPTER SIX
LONELY

East Lexington, MA
1978, Age 7

It's a long walk home from school when it's this cold out. I really should have worn mittens this morning when I left but I always think it's warmer outside than it is. At least at first, I'm right. It's okay when I'm walking down my long hill. It flattens and drops like a rollercoaster so I forget about the cold for a while. By the time I reach the flat, main road, it's too far away from home to return for anything I've forgotten. I tilt my forehead away from the wind, burying my chin inside my turtleneck top. If it's really cold, I lose my face right up to the bridge of my nose in that cloth hideaway. My hands, my poor, bare, slender hands.

Even though I'm only seven, I don't have the baby fat on my arms and hands that most kids my age do. Mommy tells me that I have Gramma Cree's hands. They were beautiful, she says. Elegant. Graceful. Just like mine. Mommy has stubby fingers.

She's glad I didn't inherit those from her. But her hands stay warmer in the winter than mine so right now I don't want elegant hands. Really, I just want my mittens. My coat pockets have holes in them and my wrists keep feeling the cold sneaking through that unfortunate space between my sleeve and the pocket. My arms are crazily long, like a giraffe's neck, so all my sleeves creep up on me. That's what Mommy says. I know we don't go shopping a lot. But we haven't moved in a year so things must still be okay. I'd like to stay at this school for a while. The teachers are nice.

I wish they had a bus, though. It takes me more than thirty minutes to walk to school. The walk home always seems to take longer, mostly because I often make stops along the way. I'm not in such a rush on the way home. Except when it's cold. Then I want to be home. Or somewhere warm, anyway.

There's an old man who is lonely after his wife died. He lives right on the main street in a little yellow house with big stairs that lead up to his front door. Mommy says that it's nice that I stop to talk to him on my way home. Sometimes he gives me cookies and candy out of his candy dish. It's a pretty dish. I wonder if his wife used to fill it before she died? Maybe he misses that about her? I wonder what else he misses?

My grandparents live far away; the ones I know, anyway. We don't have any family here. It's just Mommy and me, and now my half-sister, too, after she moved in last year. We shared a room in our old apartment. This apartment has three bedrooms so I get my own room again. She's happy about that, too. She didn't like sharing a room with her little sister. I like playing with Barbie dolls and she likes to read. I can't make them talk and do stuff when she's around.

I see the yellow house up ahead. There are four houses just like it before the yellow house but they aren't yellow like his. I play lots of games as I walk. Counting games. Counting time. Counting mailboxes. Counting cracks in the sidewalk. Counting squirrels and birds and other animals I see. I see how many things I can count in a row before I get home. I see patterns in things and I focus on them like Mommy focuses on the numbered sheets she brings home from work. They have lines and numbers printed on them and holes on each side of the paper. Mommy likes counting, too.

As I walk up his outside stairs, I start to hope that his house is warmer than it is out here. A lot warmer. Maybe he will have hot chocolate today? No. He never gives me things to drink. It's usually just the candy that's in his kitchen in the back of the house. He has me sit on the couch waiting for him to return with the sparkly dish. I like the butterscotch ones the best. The wrappers are so crinkly. If I'm careful, I can suck on one all the way home and finish it just as I reach my front door. That's even better than the counting games sometimes because I'm thinking about something that happening on the inside of me instead of out there in the noisy world.

The old man answers the door quickly after the doorbell makes the buzzing sound. I wonder if he saw me walking up the stairs? I rush inside so that all the cold air doesn't follow me. He tells me to take off my coat and have a seat while he gets the dish. I do as I'm told. He returns with the dish and I take a butterscotch and slip it in my coat pocket for later and unwrap a caramel for now. As I chew, he goes to other side of the room to the big bookshelf and pulls a small book down. He tells me that my older sister might enjoy it. She visited once with me last year but now that she goes to the junior high school, she doesn't walk home with me anymore. She gets a bus. Maybe she can read this new book, "Of Mice and Men," on that toasty warm bus. Lucky.

I set the book on my coat so I don't forget it. I say, "thank you."

As I turn back to face the old man he throws his arms around me and hugs me so hard I feel like I can't get the air back in my lungs. His fingers are laced in my long, blonde hair and his hot, heavy breath is making my ear and neck feel damp. Suddenly, I'm on the ground. He's on top of me with his face pressed against mine. His lips and tongue find mine and he's smashing my nose with his own. His body is shifting and pushing hard on me, his hands finding their way up and down me. I can't move. I can't breathe. I don't know what to do with my arms so they lay pinned to the floor. He lifts his face from mine and slides it into my neck and whispers in my ear, "Is this how you like it?"

"Mmhmm."

He grunts and moans and rolls off of me. I scurry toward my coat, straightening my dress and hair as I make my way to the door. The book falls to the floor as I scramble to get my coat back on and zipped up.

"Don't forget to give your sister the book."

I promise. I'll make sure she gets the book.

The cold air hits my face but my cheeks are so red and hot I welcome the contrast. Once I'm back on the sidewalk, I reach into my pocket for my butterscotch. My stomach is tight. I'm walking faster than I can remember walking. Crinkle crinkle goes the candy wrapper. I put the candy in my mouth. Chomp. I don't want it in my mouth after all. I shred it with my teeth and swallow the jagged pieces as fast as I can. There's no candy game today. I don't want to be in my mouth today. One, two, three, four...so many cracks in the sidewalk. So many squares still to walk before my doorstep.

I don't like it like this. Not one tiny bit.

~

Oh, Bridget,

It's not your fault.

You didn't make this happen.

It's not you.

I know that last one is the hardest to believe. You've been violated so much already that you can't imagine that you're not the common thread. Your world is built around believing that this happens to you because it's about you. You're dirty and desirable. You're slutty and sexy. You're a vixen not a victim.

That's a bunch of bullshit. The only glimmer of truth in any of that is because you've had your boundaries shattered, or frankly, never had any to begin with, you don't take any measures to protect yourself against sick bastards who violate you with ease. Like a hunter and his prey, they sniff you out, targeting you because you've separated from the pack. You're alone and vulnerable. You're an easy target.

That doesn't make it about you. That doesn't mean anything about your worth and value as a person, as a woman.

The problem is that it's happened so much already that you've come to believe that this is yours to own. You're seven years old and you think your body doesn't belong to you. You think you're here to serve other people and their sick desires.

It's a mind fuck of magnificent proportions: You're both incredibly desirable and completely insignificant. You're the object of their deepest desires yet you are invisible to them. It's no wonder you slide into their clutches over and over again. They provide you with the highest highs and the lowest lows. You really don't know what healthy relationships look like. Your life is rich with perverted examples of love and caregiving and attention.

This confusion is going to be one of your greatest heartaches over the years. You'll get into a couple of clearly abusive relationships, but more will occupy that excruciating grey area where you'll twist your psyche into a pretzel trying to see black and white. I'm so sorry; clarity is elusive.

You know what's clear? This guy was a broken, harmful man who hurt you to ease his own suffering. He was dead wrong for touching and kissing you. He had no right to be anything but grandfatherly to you, if you can even conceive of what that means. He should have kept his distance from you. Your kindness should not have come at a cost, and certainly not this one. If he had urges to treat you like this, he should have gotten mental health treatment. It's a sickness and it wasn't yours.

You know what else? Your mother should have seen this. I know you're a gifted actress but I know you also wear your heart on your sleeve. She was too consumed by survival and her own mental health issues to notice your suffering. That was unfair and also wasn't your fault. Her inability to notice you and take care of you has absolutely no bearing on your worth as a little girl. You unequivocally deserve to be loved, protected, and healed. Adults around you should be looking out for you, not the other way around. They should be making sure you don't get hurt, not hurting you. They should be ensuring you aren't neglected, not neglecting you.

You are not forgotten. I see you. I love you. I know who you are and what you are capable of. And I'm not the only one. You will meet people along your journey who will give you a different idea about who you are and what real caring looks like. They will remind you of your potential and will give you permission to demand more from others because you deserve it. You are powerful, my dear, and you will use this pain and confusion to help to heal others. Why? Because that's what you do. Even in his horrific house, your essence was to give of yourself, to be kind and loving. That is who you are: beautiful. His ugliness does not make you ugly. On the contrary. It actually shines a warm, bright light on your grace and strength.

~ Love, Me

CHAPTER SEVEN

TURTLE

East Lexington, Massachusetts
1978, Age 7

We live in a hilly neighborhood with lots of houses that fit lots of people. If my arms were longer I'll bet I could stand between two houses and touch both. That would be fun. Maybe when I get older I can do that! Our street ends on the big, busy street below, the one that leads into Boston where Mommy works. There are lots of stores on that street and even more cars.

My best friend, Lee, lives right across the street from me. She goes to a different school because we live in different towns. I think that's so neat. There's a town line that we can't see, but it's there and it keeps us apart.

Lee lives with her dad. I think her Mommy left but she never talks about that so I don't either. I know how it feels to have a parent who isn't there. She has a daddy and a turtle. I don't know who I like less, but they both keep to themselves. Their house, well, half-house, smells of animals, stale cigarettes, and stinky beer. Kind of like my house but Mommy doesn't smoke cigarettes. Not that kind anyway.

There are some other kids on our street that I sometimes play with. About five houses down (on my side, not Lee's, so they belong to my town) is a family with eight kids. They live with just their dad, too. Sometimes I wish I knew what that was like.

The house with all the kids smells worse than Lee's, but the smells are the same. Their house is always dark, like the sun can't find its way in. I know it can't rain inside but it feels like it just did. I think I have water on my skin when I am in there and I leave feeling all sticky and short of breath. Their backyard is as filled up as the house with stuff. There's even a broken car and machines that belong in the kitchen.

The oldest daughter is in high school and has a job at Kentucky Fried Chicken up the street. I know they have yummy chicken but they also sell some of the best chocolate chip cookies on the planet. Oh, and those sweet biscuits. With Mommy working all day and going to school all night, I have a lot of time to spend in my neighborhood.

I knock on the front door and the father answers, telling me that my friend was in the shower getting ready for work. To kill some time, he invites me out back where he was working on a project in that tiny excuse for a yard. Not having a father in my life, I can hardly contain my excitement to be a part of his efforts, regardless of their nature. Wearing those cheap dark blue cotton working man's pants and a mechanic's shirt, he leans down to tell me that he has a surprise for me. I can smell the liquor on his smoky breath, an aroma as familiar to me as apple pie to Norman Rockwell painting inhabitants.

"I have a pet turtle. Do you want to play with him?"

I fail to see his eyes. I'm looking at the ground.

"Sure."

With that permission, he takes my delicate hand and slips it beneath his belted pants.

As my fingers trace some soft, protruding flesh, he whispers, "that's it. He likes to have his head patted. Coax him out of his shell. That's it. You're so good with him. How do you like him?"

I mutter something polite and complimentary. Why can't I see his turtle and why is he hiding it in his trousers? There's a heaviness in the air that I can't identify at first. It grows and becomes increasingly familiar. A sickening feeling rises in my guts and washes over me like sudden nausea. I feel dirty and stupid.

I think, *not again, you filthy whore.*

As I stroke him, his silence gives way to my thoughts. How had I encouraged this? Why do I keep finding myself pleasuring men like this? What the hell is wrong with me? Can't I just be a good girl?

Just then, I hear the snapping of the cheap screen door behind us, producing one of his sons. I yank my hand from him and escape down the driveway trying to leave my memory of the moment where it took place.

Ten minutes later, after scurrying to the comfort of that main road that provided abundant distractions, I find myself in front of my friend, who had been at KFC all along, savoring the sweetness of a freshly-baked cookie in my turtle-stroking appendage.

~

Oh, Baby Girl.

I am so, so very sorry.

You've had to try to make sense of things that just can't be unraveled and put neatly back together. I want to tell you how wrong that man was for violating your tender body like that; for forever imprinting his sickness onto your wounded soul. He had no right to be near you, let alone using you to bring on his own pleasure. To draw you into his twisted world where you absorbed the message that your value was based on what you could do for others. The implication that you don't matter. That your curiosity can and will be used against you in a court of lawlessness. You're settling into the framework that you are a sexually-provocative and promiscuous girl; that you have drawn these men to you and you are responsible for your own mistreatment. That they can't help themselves. That it's not them, it's you.

It's not you, Honey.

I know you feel that, and I know where it comes from. And it's all upside down. In years to come, you'll learn that this is what abusers do. They create conditions where you end up taking responsibility for their actions. Your mom set you up for this, as you'll see. She told you that you drew out the plan for your life and assigned you control over everything that happens to you. She told you that you've asked for everything that you get. That you're in charge of the script of your life.

You're seven years old. You don't know how young and powerless you are.

Yet, let me let you in on a little secret.

You also don't know how old and powerful you are.

You are growing more powerful every day. With each violation, you hurt more deeply, I know. You take it as further evidence that no one is going to take care of you, that you're destined to a life of pain. That this is what you deserve. But I know you. I see the fire inside of you. I see your fight, your fierceness. You are an old soul, my love, and your quest is to shake loose the pain that others foist upon you and to live your truth of joy and love. To commit to find healing when you can't even see the light.

There will come a day when you will release this moment to the ethers, seeing clearly that his damaged, broken spirit is not yours to take the heat for. That this was his pain, shared with you, and had little to do with you. Your only part in this was the piece of your beautiful heart that has always wanted to make other people feel happy and comfortable, and to feel loved. He saw your tender heart and he took advantage of it. I am so sad to have to tell you this, but he will not be the last to do this. There will be more. Some will do it like this, some will do it in more subtle ways. It will continue to be excruciating so you'll numb out. Or you'll absorb it all and want to die to escape the inner torment that takes hold of your soul.

You won't do this for long.

You keep getting stronger, more loving, and increasingly grateful for the joys that so many people around you take for granted. Pain has been your close companion for as long as you can remember so when joy comes, you ride that bitch for as long and as hard as you can. This will be your saving grace. Hold onto that when times get tough. Protect your sweet heart, but don't lock it up. There are those who will be your protectors, despite your fierce outward independence. They will see through your attempts to be the girl who can do it all on her own. Keep those people close. They are your tribe.

Rest assured, you will be loved. You will be honored. You will be healed. That, my dear, is your choice and your destiny. I remain so proud of you.

You are powerful.

~ Love, Me

CHAPTER EIGHT
STRANGER

Lexington, MA
1979, Age 8

I did it! I stayed up to finish watching "Fantasy Island!" The television lights up my room in the darkness, my technicolor friend.

Mommy isn't home yet. I can see when she pulls into the driveway since my room is on the front of the house. It's a good and a bad thing since when I stay up too late she catches me in the act. She used to work all day and go to school all night, almost every night, trying to finish up college. But she finished up last year.

Now she goes out for fun. Dancing at Thackery's every Saturday night. She usually gets home after I'm asleep, but I don't like falling asleep before she gets home. My sister is in the room next to me but she doesn't make me feel safe. Mommy doesn't make me feel very safe either, but at least when she's home I know *she's* safe. I can keep track of her.

My room lights up, now from her headlights. It's a Saturday night so I don't worry about getting in trouble for being awake. She usually doesn't say anything to me anyway, not at night. I think she's just too tired from her life to care, going straight to her room and disappearing from the world, quietly.

Tonight she's not quiet. Neither is he. I don't know his name. I wonder if she does? They are laughing and talking downstairs. I can't understand what they are saying; my show is drowning them out. I'm jealous. I love Mommy's laugh. But this laugh is different. It's not her silly laugh. It's throaty. Slower. Deeper. Muffled almost. They are probably drinking. She's always drinking. Usually beer. I hate the smell of beer. It smells like sadness.

Their voices are getting closer. Quieter. They are coming upstairs. Do they think that I can't hear them? I'm 8, I'm not stupid.

They are going into her bedroom. I hate it when she brings men there. I have for as long as I can remember. I remember...

~

East Lexington, MA
1978, Age 7

The light is so beautiful in Mommy's room. It pours in from the front of the house through these windows that seem to poke out of the house. The only thing blocking the light are the sheer, lacy curtains that billow in the breeze over her enormous mattress. The doors to her room beckon me, cracked open, with the light flowing through the doors. The doors to Mommy's room have windows, too. So much light, so much to see.

It's a Saturday morning and Mommy sometimes makes pancakes on Saturday mornings so I go in to see if she's awake and in a pancake mood.

My slight body, covered by a long, lacy nightgown, wriggles through the opening between the doors. I see Mommy in bed. And another figure. They are tangled up in each other, with all of their skin shimmering in the morning light.

I must have stepped on a squeaky floorboard because they stop and right themselves to look at me. I know him. He's the married man who she followed to Boston from California. I think she was his secretary when we lived in Los Angeles. When we moved to Massachusetts and she got a new job in his company, we moved into the town he shared with his wife and daughters. They don't know about us, but I know all about them. I whisper his wife's name in my head. Such a pretty name. Like a ballerina would have. She must be so pretty.

Mommy motions with her bare arm for me to come toward them.

Reluctantly, I slowly approach the bed, stripped of sheets and covers which are draped carelessly off the foot of the bed. I see the man in all his nakedness, with his man parts laying across his upper leg. Mommy gives me a tour of his body like my friends do when they show me all their prize possessions in their rooms. Her voice is so calm, so soothing. I almost feel like she's reading me a bedtime story, only this man is here and they are both naked. After she describes where all the parts go when they are tangled up in one another, and how good it feels, she asks me if I have any questions.

How do I disappear?

~

Lexington, MA
1979, Age 8

The talking has stopped. They are whispering a little but mostly they are quiet. Until they're not. The men are usually quiet. It's not them I can hear. It's her. She moans. She whimpers. How can a person breathe so loudly that she can be heard a room away. But she's not really a room away, is she? Our closets connect. I'm hearing her through the closets. I wish the walls were soundproof. The moaning won't stop. I know her cadence and rhythm like I know the songs we sing in chorus. I hate them but I can recite them without hesitation.

Morning arrives and Mommy finds me at the kitchen table. I've been up for a short forever, still boiling inside from the happenings of the night before. My face is as magenta as her fuzzy robe, the only thing separating her soiled flesh from my gaze. She looks positively giddy. Like the cat who ate the mouse, as my teacher told us the other day. The look a person gets when they get what they want, be damned the cost others pay for it. Her hair a mess, she glances over at me before she leans down to kiss me with a cheerful "good morning!"

"Good morning? You're a whore," I seethe.

Taking a sudden step back, Mommy looks shocked by my utterance. I'm fuming, burning a hole in that smug look on her face.

"Oh, oh, mmm, mmm, oooh, oooh, ah, ah ah, mmm," I mimic. I could win an Academy Award with my convincing performance of her own slutty expressions from the night before. Once again, with some man I'd probably only meet once or twice, if at all. All that moaning must not do much to keep a man around for more than a night.

With a look of part amusement, part disapproval, Mommy mutters, "Bridget, stop it," her voice trailing off. She knows I'm spot on and doesn't appear the least bit sorry.

Fist clenched and jaw locked, I slam my ceramic bowl on the wooden table, I heave my chair to the wall with my backside. I push past her, hoping she'll fight me so I'll have even more reason to hit her, hard.

"I hate you, Mommy! I HATE you!"

I really do hate her right now, more than I ever imagined hating anyone in my whole life. She's disgusting and she doesn't even care. All I can think is, "what kind of mother IS she?"

As if she can read the condemning thought tearing through my mind, Mommy demands, "You go to your room right now, young lady! I suggest you spend some time considering why you picked me to be your mother if you were just going to hate me. That seems like a pretty silly choice. Maybe you think about that for a while."

That woman has never made any mystery of her thoughts about how we all got here. We choose our parents. We choose our obstacles. We choose our lessons and experiences. We choose our pain, ahead of time and all along the way.

Me? I chose a father who would beat and rape my mother in front of me. I chose a father who would beat and rape me. I chose a drug-addicted, disabled, unemployed father who would be my primary caretaker. I chose a mother who would stay with him, for years. I chose a mother who would send me to him to visit with him and his new common-law wife a plane flight away. I chose a mother who would move me 3,000 miles away from my family, leaving us to fend for ourselves without anyone to turn to or spend time with while she worked, studied, partied, and passed out in a drunken stupor. I chose a felon father who would be in jail more than he was free; who would only call when he needed something in jail; who would disappear from my life for years at a time with no explanation. I chose a mother who would grow marijuana in the backyard and smoke it in the house, inviting me to share it with her whenever the urge struck her. Leaving me paranoid that she might be caught and I would end up in foster care or in a group home. I chose a mother who would invite strangers home with her and have loud sex with her a few feet from her young daughters. I chose a mother who tells me freely that she never really wanted to be a mother in the first place.

I chose a mother who would confront me with these things and foist them upon me as my own choices. Not hers, mine. Not his, mine. Not theirs, mine.

Caught in the bind of turning the anger I had at my caretakers for being lousy at their jobs right back onto me for making bad choices. For wanting this. For asking for this. For wishing it into reality.

I chose this life.

The power and the pain of this overwhelms me.

I have the impressive power to choose my life, yet I have chosen to be in excruciating pain.

What kind of monster does that? What kind of crazy person chooses this existence only to resent others for her own, misguided choices? My poor parents, having a daughter who cannot be accountable to them for her lousy judgment.

What the hell was I thinking?

~

Oh, Bridget,

You amaze me.

You're eight years old and you distinguish between irresponsible and responsible behavior already. And what's more? You call it out, against adults even. You are bold and your voice is gaining fortitude. It will be tested many times because the adults around you, especially your mom, refuse to take responsibility for their own actions and the risks and injuries you suffer as a result. You're going to see how fucked up things are but your observations will fall on deaf ears. You're solidifying your position as the scapegoat, Honey, and this will be irrevocably painful. You'll cut yourself off from the tribe and you'll stand alone in your certainty that you deserve better.

You do. You absolutely do.

You're already learning that other people's actions have more to do with them than they have to do with you. You're honing your insight, your gift of a sixth sense. It will serve you well and you will help countless people along the way. You have this innate ability to cut right through the bullshit of any given moment and define the deeper issue. It's no small wonder. You've been studying people, trying to anticipate their next move, seeking to understand them, your entire life. It's how you've survived.

You see your mother pretty clearly. She's damaged and desperate for male attention. Her needs will always come first, even when she claims how much she's giving to you. She is giving you love, don't get me wrong, but her drive to be a perpetual martyr and drama queen will always trump whatever you need. Even her friends will see you as the adult figure in the relationship. She does her best, she'll tell you, but this message will grow weaker and weaker over time. She has some amazing qualities, but like so many others among us, her disease of addiction and mental incapacities will cast a dark shadow over all the aspects you want so desperately to love and trust.

Know this: She will __always__ choose a man over you. You don't deserve this. You deserve to be protected. But you won't be, time and time again. This is teaching you a great deal about humanity, my dear. You are starting to see that those who claim to love you the most can (and often will) hurt you the most. You can comprehend that there is good and bad in everyone, it's just a matter of degree and circumstance.

This crap with men in her bedroom will fuck you up good for a long, long time. When you become sexually active, you'll hold her example of what not to do. You'll stay quieter than a church mouse, and for reasons that originate in trauma throughout your childhood, your ability to let go with anyone will frustrate you for decades to come. Your mother's inability or unwillingness to protect you from, and worse, her predilection to expose you to, sexual abuse will stay with you.

The shadow cast is long and wide.

Know that you are right to be angry. I wish I could find a way to remove that audio file from your brain so that it wouldn't soil your own intimacy later on, but I'm no genie. You're going to have to do that all on your own, unfortunately, like so many other journeys you'll walk solo. Go easy on yourself. Rome wasn't built in a day and neither were you. Exorcising some of these demons will be hard work. It'll be slow progress, and when you face a jackass in the bedroom, you'll lose ground you'll fear you may never regain.

Hold tight, little lady. You are better than that. You're not handing over your power for too long. It'll take a while, no doubt, but you will rise up. You are worthy of respect. You are entitled to joy. You are beautiful and full of potential. You are powerful.

~ Love, Me

REMEMBER THE LOTUS FLOWER

Great people will always be mocked by those
Who feel smaller than them.
A lion does not flinch at laughter coming from a hyena.
A gorilla does not budge from a banana thrown at it by a
monkey.
A nightingale does not stop singing its beautiful song
At the intrusion of an annoying woodpecker.
Whenever you should doubt your self-worth,
remember the lotus flower.
Even though it plunges to life from beneath the mud,
It does not allow the dirt that surrounds it
To affect its growth or beauty.
Be that lotus flower always.
Do not allow any negativity or ugliness
In your surroundings
Destroy your confidence,
Affect your growth,
Or make you question your self-worth.
It is very normal for one ugly weed
to not want to stand alone.
Remember this always.
If you were ugly,
Or just as small as they feel they are,
Then they would not feel so bitter and envious
Each and every time they are forced
To glance up at magnificently
Divine YOU.
~ Suzy Kasseem

CHAPTER NINE

BREAKFAST

Lexington, Massachusetts
1981, Age 9

The morning sun shines into my windows, pushing me out of my sleepy state. It's a Saturday morning so I could lounge in bed for hours but I never do. I'm an early bird, getting up with the sunrise, which makes me very unpopular at sleepovers. My friends are always sleeping and I lay awake, trying not to make a sound so they can sleep as late as they need to. It's a tie between my rumbling tummy and my restless mind as to what is responsible for stirring the others awake long before they are ready.

I can't help myself. My mind rarely stops so I find it incredibly hard to relax. I've used it to my advantage recently, though. When I go to my friend Susan's house, I use the early morning hour to quell one of my many compulsions: Cleaning. She lives with her two big (and super messy) brothers and her mom who works full-time and is in a band. She is the coolest mom ever. Susan doesn't always say so, but I think she knows how good she has it. I'm usually up hours before the rest of the house and I get so bored. There's only so much HBO a girl can watch.

So, in my incredible ingenuity, I struck a deal. I clean the common areas of the house (bathrooms, kitchen, living room, etc.) and I keep whatever spare change I find along the way. It's genius! They get a clean house with all their laundry picked up, dishes done, food put away, surfaces scrubbed, and everything that I can do quietly, and I get to clean (which I love to do) and make money!

Plus, it kinda makes me feel like I'm part of the family. Like I have a role. I don't fit in with them, that's for sure. They are cool and I am not. They are light and confident and speak their minds. I'm scared and sad and unsure of everything about myself. I make mistakes constantly. I hide in the light as much as I can. But when I clean for them I'm useful. And they have such a gorgeous house; it's just begging to be tidy. Tidy lets in more light.

Today I'm at home, though. I'll clean some, I'm sure, but I won't get paid for it.

I head downstairs to get some breakfast. If it's a good day for Mommy, she will be up making pancakes. If it's a bad day, I'll eat cereal. My sister sleeps late and hates breakfast anyway. She won't notice Mommy. That's my job. A job that has a funny way of paying me.

I'm alone in the kitchen. Our two cats wander around my feet, meowing to tell me they are as hungry as I am. I pet them one by one, their tails swirling between my fingers. They purr with delight, knowing what's coming next. Food. I am always here to take care of them. They know they can count on me. As I empty the soft food into their bowls, they scurry to consume it, barely noticing my presence now.

There's still no sign of Mommy. I don't want to go back upstairs to check on her, afraid of what I'll find.

She fights the sad, except when she invites it in. Then it envelops her. On Saturday mornings, I watch that animal show where the scientists tell you all about what each tail snap and ear wiggle means from each species. Are they mad? On alert? About to mate? If you watch closely enough you can predict their next move.

I do that with Mommy. I study her relentlessly. She reveals herself without opening her mouth. She has such sad eyes. Big, brown, and mourning something that you can't quite define. Always on the verge of tears, she's so fragile, so broken, so deeply injured. She talks about faith in the unknown and the strength of positive thinking.

But still, she wants to die.

I hear her creaky door open and I sigh deeply.

We made it another day.

She coasts down the stairs leading into the kitchen, wrapped in her long and fuzzy burgundy robe. She looks empty. Like she isn't inside herself.

It's a bad Mommy morning.

Cue: Bridget.

I race over to her, sharing my sweetest smiles, and give her a soft bear hug, trying to heal her from the outside in. I seem to squeeze the tears out, finding her sobbing as I step back from her. She smears the liquid draining from her nose across her face, sniffling some of it back in. I tell her how pretty she is and how much I love her. I give her kisses on her wet cheeks.

"I'm sorry, Baby. Mommy is sad. I was going to kill myself last night but I didn't. I knew I promised you pancakes this morning and I didn't want to break my promise."

She lived because of my breakfast. Because of her promise to take care of me.

Will that be enough tomorrow? She doesn't make breakfast on any other morning. What will carry her through tomorrow? I have to find something that will tie her to the dawn. Something that will bring her through the dark night. I'm not enough, but I have to find a way to be. To be what she lives for, every day. I visit the vitamin drawer every morning, taking out her epilepsy pills and counting them one by one. I know that if she takes too many she could die. As I pull the bottle out, I gingerly shake it, hoping it feels as full as it did the day before. If it's full, she's likely to be alive up there in her room.

What would I do if she was gone? Where would I go? It wouldn't matter where I went, how far I traveled: I'd take my failure with me.

Killing my mother would mark my life forever. Not much out there worse than that. Shameful. Just like me.

~

Oh, Bridget,

You were made to believe that you could save your parents from their demons. That if you were cute enough, talented enough, smart enough, any old kind of enough, they would be happy. They would be healthy. You could fix them. They would stop drinking. They'd stop using drugs. They'd stop being sad all the time. Daddy would stay out of jail and move to be closer to you. Mommy would stop bringing men in to fill her deep voids. I know you're not expecting some Norman Rockwell painting, but you want some degree of stability and normalcy, not just from the outside looking in. If you could just get their sadness to go away, things would be so much better. You would feel loved.

You deserve that. Oh, how much you deserve that. You are so loveable. So full of light and joy and compassion and strength. They lean on you far more than any child should ever be leaned on. They have put their very survival into your tiny hands. It's no wonder you feel overwhelmed, like a hamster on a wheel trying to move it forward but always stuck in place. Round and round you go, full of anxiety about what would happen if you stopped trying to be so heroic. But they won't let you stop. Like the sun, your light draws them near and they soak up your rays, always coming back for more no matter how weak you may feel. They are sick and they can't meet their own needs so they come knocking at your door to do that for them, to fill them up. But you can't. Not because you're not intrinsically amazing, but because they are black holes of emotional unrest. They act insane because they are shades of insane.

Life is unpredictable with them because they are unpredictable. They are unstable. You will learn in years to come that your father was likely schizophrenic and definitely depressed. His lifelong drug abuse of everything from LSD to the alternating cocktail of methamphetamines and heroin broke what was left of his mind. He makes promises he can't keep because he's not in charge of his own existence. Your mom tries her best but she is struggling to be a functioning adult let alone a single mother. Her manic depression and epilepsy zap her energy, and her self-medicating with alcohol, pot, and men just covers it up for a moment. If all of these vices can't help them, nothing can until they decide to get help. To go into therapy. To join a recovery program. To take charge of their own lives.

I'm going to tell you a secret that I wish could help you to let go of this yoke around your neck:

They won't make any of those choices.

They will die depressed and just as addicted as they are today. You'll have tried every trick in your arsenal and none will make a difference. It'll take you years and almost cost you your life but you'll extricate yourself from their crazy mess. You'll stop feeling responsible for their sanity and recovery. You'll pull yourself into a psychological bubble that will insulate you from their burdens. You will be free, my love. You will not succumb to their DNA or their undue influence. You will be your own person, living by your own rules and definitions. You are powerful. You are more than your heritage. You are magically, wonderfully you.

~ Love, Me

BACKSTORY TWO
RAISED BY WOLVES

力

"People forget years and
remember moments." ~ Ann Beattie

~

There's no other way to say it: I was raised to be abused. I put
myself in harm's way over and over again and no one stepped
in to protect me. No one blinked an eye at the peril I was in so
it seemed normal and acceptable to me. Two adults picked me
up hitchhiking when I was five years old. *Five years old?*
Doesn't that seem crazy? But it wasn't crazy in my world. If it
wasn't okay someone would have said something...done
something...right? People treated me like a grown up so I
interacted with adults like one. I took the ownership over
events like adults do, to my perpetual detriment. They took
advantage of me but I didn't see it that way back then. I saw

85

myself as their equal so how could they have taken advantage of me? I allowed it, invited it, accepted it.

Yet, it wasn't my permission to offer.

When I was in college, friends were perplexed by the repetition of these violating experiences. How could this happen so much to one little girl? Easy: I was a walking, talking target. I was a little girl who didn't see herself that way, sending out a beacon to every sick person in a 100-mile radius. With every abuse, I became that much more vulnerable to the next. I saw myself very differently than my peers saw themselves. My mind was overstimulated with images of sex, violence, addiction, and every other nastiness perpetrated against me. I had the body of a child but the mind of an emotionally-stunted adult in many ways.

In other words, I was ripe for the picking.

~

My mom was a single mother, working full-time in Boston while we lived in the suburbs, poised to get the best education public education could provide. She was attending Northeastern University at night to earn her undergraduate degree, leaving us alone most nights until 11pm.

We didn't have friends or family in the area so while she worked, my half-sister and I were on our own. I walked by myself the mile each way to school and back and took care of myself before and after school, sometimes taking the city bus to and from extracurricular activities starting at age 6. My half-sister was five years older than me so with the exception of my first grade year, we never went to the same school so she didn't walk with me. Like so many kids of the 70s and 80s, we were often left to fend for ourselves.

I felt very capable being this independent and figured out ways to blend in whenever possible. On half-days at school I would often walk a mile to the bus station, take a bus to the train station, then take two trains to get to my mom's stop in downtown Boston. On the bus and trains I would spot an elderly person and sit next to them, quietly. If they exited, I would get up with them and then find another and sit down with them. I assumed people would think that I was their grandchild and leave me alone. The fact that I trusted adults even after my neighbors violated me demonstrates my frame of mind.

You see, I saw the sexual contact we shared as consensual.

After getting off the subway downtown, I would walk a few blocks to her office and spend the afternoon at her desk doing filing and matching statements with the accounting ledger. Sometimes I would leave her office and walk a few blocks to Fanuiel Hall to window shop while she finished working. I felt incredibly grown up and this made me so happy. Despite the danger, these were among my fondest memories.

I might have seen the future unfold more quickly if I'd been more fearful in general. Forty-something-year-old me would have sensed the evil dripping from my molesters' tongues, but seven-year-old me still held onto what was left of my naivete. Sadly, innocence had long since left my little body.

"Stranger Danger" came to our schools long after I came of age. Though, it wouldn't have saved me from this particular grief. These men were neighbors. The man with the turtle was a neighbor, a parent, a familiar person. Which made him that much more dangerous. Unlike the old man with the candy, this man occupied a house I entered to play with my friends. It was full of children. By those loose standards, it was safe.

I don't know that I ever knew a damn thing about trust, but even if I had, I probably would have been inclined to trust these man, at least initially. I know that being in those houses made me feel dark and dirty, but I didn't have the sense to avoid them. Nothing scared me, perhaps because I'd already seen stark views of the evil side of humanity. What could be worse than what I'd already seen? I was comfortably numb.

Given the connection I felt to the positive threads in these stories – the food at KFC and the candy at the old man's house – it's no small wonder I have a fascination with sweets to this day. They bring me comfort in a closet-binge-eater sort of way. My years as a bulimic and anorectic centered around my consumption of cookies and candy. The only difference from my early KFC experience was the level of secrecy. I flaunted my sweet tooth back then. As the years went on, I hid my obsession. I would buy – and sometimes steal – candy and cookies and indulge in them, hidden from the world. In my teens I consumed boxes, not individual cookies, at a time.

Turtles? My skin crawls at the sight of them, particularly when their heads wander in and out of their shells, seeking something I can't quite label. The air in the room changes, leaving me short of breath, wiping a substance from my hands that never, ever disappears. Reading "Of Mice and Men" in high school was torture.

On the heels of these neighbor abuses, my mom, sister, and I moved to another neighborhood up the road after our house was condemned for a roach infestation. If you've ever opened a kitchen cabinet and had a sea of roaches pour out onto the counter like we did, you have my deepest sympathies.

Almost forty years later, I drove to the neighborhood, stunned how poignant and accurate my vivid memories of the area was, right down to the spacing between the houses and the distance I walked in my explorations. Everything was exactly as I'd remembered it. If I was an artist I could have painted an exact replica of each scene. The accuracy of my memories was deeply reassuring. I hadn't imagined these things. They were real.

More than anything, I needed to know that my pain was anchored in reality.

~ Freedom versus Power ~

Some would call my mother's approach "progressive" and all about "sexual freedom." Perhaps if I had never been raped or molested before, these experiences might not have been as jarring as they were. But they were. To me, they were traumatic. They drove me to have a highly conflicted relationship with sex, one marked by both obsession and repulsion. So much in my world was sexually charged, teaching me that sexual urges were dominant and pervasive. That sex sometimes accompanied love, but usually it was used as an outlet for and a source of power.

Power that could be wielded over me.

Power I could wield over others.

The road to seeing it as connecting and real was long and rocky because the sick scaffolding was firmly placed.

From a ridiculously young age, my mom counted on me to be her confidante and supporter. When I was ten, she took me to a therapist to deal with my anxiety. During the intake session, I shared with the therapist my knowledge all of the monthly bills that we had including their amounts and due dates and the likelihood that we could pay them. I knew how much my mom earned, the support she received from her father, ex-husbands, and what she had in the bank. I knew her credit card limits and the full story of her previous foreclosures with her two ex-husbands.

I knew at age six how many stab wounds it took for the robber who murdered my great aunt to snuff out her life.

I knew how many marijuana plants she had in the backyard.

I knew how to roll a good joint.

I knew her height, weight, bra size, and waist circumference. I knew every freckle, hair, and dimple on her naked body.

I knew that she saw tiny Mexicans wearing sombreros dancing on her belly when she took certain drugs.

I knew that men told her that her jiggly ass was attractive, especially when she shook it madly, on and off stage.

I knew how many men she'd slept with, the social diseases she'd contracted and from who. I knew when she was having a genital herpes breakout, how many days it lasted, and how much discomfort she was in.

I knew the approximate girth and length of my father's penis and the frequency of his sexual demands and how sore it left her.

I knew that they both loved porn, between my father's requests for it in jail and that our bookshelves even now that were flanked with cartoon and regular porn.

I knew many detailed stories of the beatings and rapes we endured at my father's hands.

I knew which teeth my father knocked out of her mouth and where she kept the false tooth retainer she wore for years before she got implants.

~ Rollercoasters ~

My mom's epilepsy vied for as much attention as her mental illness. Try as I might, I could never find the pattern between her mania, depression, and seizure activity. One thing you could count on with my mom was that you never knew what you were going to get with her.

She might be heartbreakingly sad. Or freakishly excitable and energetic. She could bring the brightest, sunniest day or withdraw into a sad, fragile little girl. She was rarely anything in between.

When she was up, I thought it was my job to be up with her, whether that meant singing crazy songs and dancing around the house or readily accompanying her on her "going crazy" trips to who knows where. When she was feeling spunky she would approach me out of nowhere and say, "I'm goin' crazy, wanna come along?" and I'd hop in the car for an adventure. We might be going to the grocery store or the fast-food drive thru, but she would spice it up by going a different route or singing in the car along the way. I'm not sure why, but we never took these trips with my half-sister, even though she was living with us at the time. I suppose it was just another example of a connection that just we shared, a way that I knew our mother differently than she ever did, for the good and the bad.

My mom had a never-ending to do list. Always. She believed if she hadn't completed a project it would be enough of an incentive not to kill herself. So she kept projects partially done perpetually. Me? I felt like a hamster on a wheel, running faster and faster but never getting anywhere. I had to perform, succeed, measure up at all costs. It was exhausting but I couldn't stop or someone I loved might die.

My mom continually refused therapy or medication for her mental illness. She had been in a psychiatric hospital in college as the result of a breakdown she had in her junior year. While she was in the hospital, they did electroshock treatment for her epilepsy and manic depression. The drugs she they gave her made her not feel like herself. She used to sing me a song that one of the other patients sang over and over and over and over again as she rocked back in forth in her chair.

"Good morning to you. Good morning to you. We're all in our places with bright shining faces."

She didn't return to complete her education until she was in her 30s, following the path of marriage and motherhood instead. She also never went to a therapist again either.

Fast forward twenty years. She called me, telling me she wanted to kill herself. By that time, I had children of my own, people who depended on me. I told her to get help. Call a therapist. Dial up the suicide hotline. Get on meds.

She refused it all. Again. She had an excuse for every suggestion I offered. I told her that I couldn't be her sounding board anymore. I needed all of my resources to be the best mom I could be. I couldn't be hers anymore. If she wasn't willing to get help, then deal with it. I hoped she wouldn't make a fatal decision but it was hers to make. I was done trying to save her when she was unwilling to make the necessary shifts to make her life different. She lived her life wanting to die.

She eventually succeeded.

At 69 she drank herself to death, launching herself into full kidney failure and a stroke that left her brain dead.

My fears were finally realized; my worrying could finally end.

She was free, and so was I.

CHAPTER TEN
BACK

力

Lexington, MA
1980, Age 8

It's amazing what you can do with a circle and square cake pan and some frosting. Mommy and I spent all morning putting it together. I love making fun things in the kitchen, with or without Mommy. I feel like a big girl when I do.

The cake looks just like a cat with a big circle face and little triangle ears and whiskers made of black licorice. Our two cats, Midnight and Hawthorne, are turning one today so I invited some of my best friends over for a cats' birthday party. The "pin the tail on the cat" game is a big hit as long as I can get Alice to stop chasing Hawthorne (my sister's cat) around with the fake tail! She's so crazy. You can hear shrieks all over the house at a pitch only possible from eight-year-old, sugar-infused girls.

Somewhere in the distance I hear our phone ring. My mom answers and speaks in the kitchen to someone, I don't know who. Her tone is different from when she talks to BeBe (her best girlfriend) or Bob-noxious (my pet name for some guy who is totally crushing on my mom and could talk for hours without taking a breath).

No, it's someone else, but the shrieking from my friends is so loud I can't eavesdrop well. Where is Alice NOW? I really hope she doesn't catch my cat, for the cat's sake and hers.

Claws hurt when they pierce your flesh.

I turn the corner into the living room and my mom is standing before me. The look on her face is familiar but I can't place it. Cautionary, sprinkled with joy.

"That was your dad. He will call back later, after the party is over," Mommy shares.

Daddy? It's been at least two years since I've heard from him. I feel butterflies in my tummy, downright giddy at the thought that he was back. Could it be true? Could he be coming back?

I can hardly contain my excitement for the rest of the party, with each guest's departure spurring a giggle of what was to come. As we clean up from the party, I listen closely for the phone to ring. It was like Christmas Eve, only in April. Wait! It's April first. That means it's April Fools' Day. Could this all be a joke? Maybe Daddy didn't call.

I'm starting to doubt my joy.

Calm down, Bridget. It could be all pretend. It probably is.

My hands are shaking I'm so anxious for the phone to ring. What will he say? How will he explain his absence since I was six and he sent me a television for Christmas? I watch my television every day. As much as I can. Television is my closest companion. The only thing I hate about it is how that weird message and fuzz comes on in the middle of the night when I fall asleep watching it. It wakes me up sometimes and I lay there alone in my stirring thoughts, driven to near insanity obsessing about life, death, and every last thing in between. My mind conjures up every possible outcome to any situation, creating vivid imaginings of a different life, a shifted reality from my own.

Mostly, I lose myself in fantasy about Daddy coming back around.

In my fantasy, when he first sees me, he is watching me doing something amazing, looking beautiful. The perfect picture of a gifted, miraculous child that would be enough to make him want to stay this time. His disappearances leave me breathless. Sudden, and without warning, he leaves my life. It's been happening for years already and I'm only eight. I try and try but I can't detect the pattern well enough to prepare for it accurately.

Spending my early years in California, the aftershocks of an earthquake are its most predictable feature. The same goes for Daddy's disappearances. I can always count on the fallout after the fact, but there's no doorway secure enough to brace me for the tremor.

It seems like hours before Daddy calls again, collect of course. Mommy remains patient with his collect calls for some reason. Her voice gets all squeaky when she first talks to him on the phone, then it gets low and slow. She must miss him like I do. She says she will never marry another man after him, even though men come in and out of her bedroom all the time. Marriage is different, apparently, at least for Mommy.

I feel the ringing deep in my chest. The tremors return.

~

Dearest Bridget,

This day will be like déjà vu to you, even more so than it already is. As his addiction deepens and his criminal convictions multiply, he will slip out of your world unexpectedly and for long durations many more times before he stops leaving. When he's around, he'll suck you dry emotionally, leaning on you in every conceivable way, drawing you into his perpetual pity party. You will lose sight of you being his victim as he paints the world as victimizing him. You'll feel responsible for making his world better yet you'll have limited tools to really help. He will be angry at you for your limitations and will paint you as uncaring and selfish.

Not one iota of this is your fault.

You don't deserve to have a father who can't hold his shit together and who places you precariously on his roller coaster existence, a pariah on your psychic flesh.

You keep going back for more, though. Every time he disappears you're on the phone trying to track down his parole officer, back-alley drug slut, or some criminal companion. You've taken your mother's lead on this one, for sure, always looking for his bright side. Your mother was beaten handily by him for years, with false teeth implanted in her mouth as proof of his rage.

Nevertheless, until the day she dies, he is spoken of as the love of her life.

She takes him back after this phone call, reuniting with him. He lives with you for a couple of months, traveling thousands of miles to see you. It's the longest span you've spent with him since you were two and you're so hopeful that this will be long term. You look past his secretive behavior in the basement, knowing full well that he's getting high on drugs down there.

What's really screwy if you look under the hood of your psyche is that you even want him in your life in the first place. It's a result of your Freudian obsession to beat out your mother as the top recipient of his affections and his hopeful recovery. That he will do for you what he never did for her, and you'll nearly kill yourself trying to make that so. The man beat and raped you for years, from diapers to preschool, yet you work tirelessly to show him how deserving you are of his love. Stockholm Syndrome ain't got nothing on you, Sister.

You'll learn a term called "trauma bond" some years in the future and it will describe you to a "t." In the meantime, you're going to keep drinking from the poison well, hoping to concoct some magic potion to distinguish what happened to you early on to what you pray you'll receive at some undetermined point in the future.

It's a pipe dream and it's excruciating.

You're twisting yourself into a pretzel to attract the love and affection of a person who continues to abuse and abandon you, and then you're owning the blame for his failures.

This is fifteen shades of fucked up.

Don't get me wrong: It's completely understandable.

It just doesn't serve you. He's calling on you to nurture him when it should be the other way around. You weren't born to soothe him, yet, that's been your job from birth, a job that sucks you dry.

One day, many years from now, you'll volunteer in your county jail, talking to inmates about your experiences to attempt to help them come to terms with their choices and how to jump their path. One man will draw you in when you see your path in his. You'll name his struggle much the same as yours:

Choosing loyalty to a scumbag over the freedom to be happy.

Bit by bit, you'll grab onto this message and claim your independence. For now, he's holding you tightly in his grasp. He knows what he's doing, too. He writes you heartfelt letters, entertains you with witty repartee, draws you adorable pictures on the outside of every one of his prison letters, and, most importantly, he tells you how much he loves you. You're starving for his love, convinced that if he changes his ways and shows up in your life like a real father should, the past will be wiped away, with you to thank for the reincarnation.

It's all smoke and mirrors.

It'll take you another half dozen times for you to grandly tell him to fuck off and die. You'll only see him in person three more times before that fateful day, and you'll go through Hell in that span, trying to unravel the twisted threads of your relationship with him.

Someday you'll fully appreciate what spurred his return this day.

He told you that his common-law wife died.

This is truthful.

He'll tell you that she killed herself.

This is a lie.

He'll never be prosecuted for his crime due to a lack of physical evidence, but he killed her. He threw her off a bridge into a raging river. This comes as little shock to you, given your shared history. Still, owning that your father is a murderer casts doubt over your belief that you are anything but evil, nature and nurture both weighing heavily against you.

You are not evil.

You are not your father.

You are not his sins.

You did not create this mess.

You will, however, claw your way out of it.

It'll be a long and messy road, though.

Your soul pays a high price for this dance you share with him. For years to come, you'll continue to look for him in crowded streets, in passing cars, on buses and in trains, hoping you'll see his face and the longing for him will end.

You won't. It won't.

He's a mirage. He's not the man you want him to be and he never will be.

I know you, though. One of your most endearing qualities is your effervescent hope in the goodness of people, no matter how evil and twisted the rest of the world judges them to be. You see glimmers in the darkness, always. This will set you up for heartbreak, Honey, but it will also be your saving grace. This search for the good in others will allow you to see your own goodness when you start to believe that you are shit. You're not.

Sometimes, though, take my advice: When you see a steaming pile of human crap, resist the urge to dig in it to find the bright shiny object it's covering. Just walk away. Know that there's something valuable in there but you don't have to be the one to reveal it. You've got enough to do on your own to heal you. You don't need to be covered in their mess.

You are powerful.

Use your power to soothe yourself first. The stronger you are the more you can bring healing to the world. I know that is your destiny. You know that, too. It's what keeps you going when you are down and lonely. You press on because that's what you do. You are pretty fucking amazing, young lady. Keep that shit up.

~ Love, Me

Untitled (1980)
By Jerry Cannon (aka, Daddy)

"We are all asleep
And life is but a dream.
Someday we all awaken dead
To discover what livin' means.

Where does it end?
Will the hurting ever go away?
Will I live to see the day
When the crying ends?

The only way there is for me
Is to find escape in Hell
From the hell I'm in today
Only clouds can bring the rain
Only death can stop the pain.

The future is only empty years
Of loneliness and tears."

BACKSTORY THREE
SECRETS

"Cruelty is the opposite of love,
and its traumatic effect,
far from being reduced, is actually reinforced
if it is presented as a sign of love." ~ Alice Miller

~

I knew my father was a felon. A drug addict. A meth cooker. A heroin mixer. A bomb maker. A wife and child abuser. A rapist.

I also knew that my father was a murderer.

On Halloween 1979, he argued with my step-mother, Trudi, and threw her off a bridge into the rapids below. She was naked, her clothes on the embankment. They were big skinny dippers which explains her nakedness. Was he naked, too, when he killed her? I'll never know.

He reached out to my mother and me about six months later, during our cats' birthday party, after he fled to Washington State. The police in California reportedly didn't have enough physical evidence to hold him so they let him go. My mother welcomed him into our home, playing house with him for two months. They talked about getting back together for good. They slept together. Giggled in the kitchen like newlyweds.

While he was there, he gave her a key to a safety deposit box held on the West Coast that he said "held all the answers." She passed this statement and the key along to me after he died 15 years later. Even with the help of the FBI, I never located the box. Or all the answers.

Their reunion experiment failed.

My dad left for Washington State hours before her parents came from California to Boston to celebrate her graduation from Northeastern where she'd taken all those night classes to get her undergraduate degree at the age of thirty-six. They probably passed each other in the airport.

The week that my grandparents were in town was spent avoiding any mention of my father and his visit. My grandparents were footing a chunk of our bills on a monthly basis and any connection with my father would have put a quick stop to that, not to mention the utter disappointment in my mother from my grandparents. So we lied. We dodged. We tried not to slip. Being eight years old, this was easier said than done.

Here was the most monumental experience I'd had to date and I could say nothing about it. I had to leave his name out of every recent memory he'd touched. When you're a child of divorce you dream incessantly about having your parents get back together, especially when both of your parents speak of the lasting love they have for one another. And here it happened, if only briefly, and I was sworn to secrecy. I *finally* had good news to share and I couldn't speak of it.

More secrets.

While he was with us for those two months, he coached my half-sister's (my mom's daughter, not his) softball team. He even got a special team shirt and baseball hat.

My sport was ice skating and I spent hours every day at the rink practicing.

He never saw me skate.

My half-sister had been telling me since she moved back in with our mom and me when I was six (she was eleven) that I was born to replace her, adding that since she was now back it was time for me to leave. Now my own father was choosing her over me. Her father was very involved in her life and I remember thinking, "no one chooses me, not even my own father."

While he was staying with us, he watched the mail very closely. After getting packages delivered, he spent hours in the basement where he could not be disturbed, not for anything. I made the mistake of going to look for him once and as my hand touched the doorknob I heard his angry voice yell, "Noooooooooo! Stay out of here!"

I did.

I knew he was a drug addict. Even if I couldn't see him, I knew he was getting high.

Once again, my voice was only relevant in its silence.

Still, I knew too damn much too damn early. The one thing I didn't know: How to find anyone who would choose *me*. I continue to carry shreds of that with me as evidence of my invisibility and inconsequence.

CHAPTER ELEVEN
COLLECT

Lexington, Massachusetts
1980, Age 9

I don't have a number to call. I never have. Picking up the phone gets me nowhere, unless it's ringing, which it rarely does. I check it constantly, making sure it has a dial tone. He can't call if the phone is malfunctioning so I have to make sure it's always operational.

What's that saying? "A watched pot never boils." What a brain screw. I want to watch the phone so I make sure to answer it if it rings. But if I do that it won't ring? I need it to ring. More than anything in the world, I hunger for that connection, that voice on the other end of the phone.

A sign that he loves me.

More than that. A sign that I am worth loving. That I matter.

When he does call, it's never his voice that I hear at first. Instead, it's the operator. Collect calls work like that, with the operator announcing the caller so I can decide if I want to accept the charges.

That pause as she gets him on the line seems to last a short forever, my whole existence hanging in the emptiness.

What if he hangs up? What if she disconnects him? Is today a good Daddy day or a bad Daddy day? The good Daddy days are so rare but when they happen I lose myself in them. His unparalleled sense of humor, usually profane and perverted, rains down in our conversations. I let giggles escape amidst scolding him for his inappropriate innuendos.

Just hearing Daddy happy injects me with hope. Hope that someday, maybe soon, he will find his way back to me and out of the dark, twisted holes he keeps finding himself in. That he will be more than just a voice on the other end of the phone or a pen pal from 3,000 miles away. Laughter gives me hope.

The bad Daddy days offer far less fun. Those days bring a shiver to my spine, like a bitter cold February wind in New England. I can feel the darkness coming from his throat, like razors sliding off his tongue. Sadness and rage stirred together, with one rising above the other without notice.

Did I send the package he requested? Was it sent promptly and completely? Did I fill out the correct paperwork? Did I include a thoughtful, loving letter? Don't I know how lonely prison is? Can't I be bothered to do exactly as he asks? Why can't he count on me when I know that I'm the only person in the world who he can turn to?

He drills me with these questions on bad Daddy day calls, subtly sometimes, with a sad sigh and a guilty reference to how terrible things are for him behind those prison walls. How much he struggles with constant pain, how bloody and crampy his clot-filled legs are. His disorder will kill him soon enough. In the meantime, can't I just find my way to those specialty support socks and get them in the mail to him?

"Don't forget to include those pastries I love. Oh, and you have to make sure to get those magazines they keep behind the counter. 'Forum' is my favorite. Prison is lonely, Munchkin. It's been so long since I've seen my woman."

I am nine years old but I know what this means, all too well.

~

The convenience store clerk gives me such a disdainful look as I, as maturely and confidently as I can, request this month's "Forum" from the rack behind him. There is no wrapping on the periodical so its cover and content dangle in front of us making the air thick and heavy.

There is no escaping the shame I feel. Bad girls do this sort of thing. I'm a nine-year-old whore and everyone knows it, even this virtual stranger. He can see the moral slime I'm covered in. It oozes out of me every time I open my filthy mouth. The looks I get everywhere I go tell me that I do a shabby job concealing my true form.

I'm garbage and everyone knows it.

The clerk thumps the magazine on the counter in front of me, requesting payment, probably suspecting I won't have the cash. Another customer stands next to me, looking down on me with some blend of pity and distaste. I don't blame him.

I'm pathetic to the core.

I place the cash on the counter, sheepishly take my change, and slink out of the store, hearing the bell jingle as the heavy door shuts. With no bag to disguise my sinful purchase, I tuck it under my left arm so passersby can't see what I have. I've gotten so skilled at hiding things, so good at this masquerade. There are still people in my life who don't know what a wretch I really am; how unloved, dishonest, and downright trashy. I'm a thief, a liar, and a whore. No wonder my life is such a mess.

I deserve nothing more than the little that I have.

On the two-block walk home, I stop halfway at the pharmacy where they sometimes carry his special socks. I step over every crack and break in the sidewalk, hoping that I've avoided placing that curse on Daddy. You know, "step on a crack, break your mama's back. Step on a line, break your papa's spine."

Maybe that's why he suffers so much? I know I stepped on cracks when I was younger, sometimes out of anger, often just to see how powerful I truly was. Neither Mommy nor Daddy ever suffered a broken back or spine but maybe the fates torment my parents differently.

Maybe me stepping on those cracks shattered their minds and hearts.

Support socks and dirty magazines can't fix that. Cigarette cartons and pastries do little to mask it. I have to hurry home so I can get Daddy's package together. No telling how long it will take to get the right box to fit everything he's requested. Certain I'll fail him somehow, no matter how hard I try, I consider hiding in my room and pretending the package project away.

I do that sometimes. I get lost in other distractions. I do kid stuff. I watch a lot of television. So much television. I don't wish myself into the shows so much as I forget that there is anything except the show. My reality fails to exist. I escape and nothing in this reality means anything. My private technicolor nirvana. Everything is so different for the characters but what I like most is how neat everything is.

Things begin and end. Resolutions occur. Tidiness reigns. My messy life overwhelms me. So I check out. Often. For extended periods of time. Indecision rules me and confirms my permanent status as a loser. How can I amount to anything if I can't even get out of bed? No wonder I'm such a klutz. Everyone at school makes fun of me during gym class. I think I'm the only kid in the history of time to strike out at kickball. How can a person miss a kickball? I do, often. I miss at lots of things. Often. My mind is as worthless as my legs, as my everything.

~

Dear Bridget,

You deserve so much more than the scraps you beg for.

Your father keeps fucking his life up, over and over again. You keep drawing him into yours, taking whatever shred of himself he's willing to toss over the fence to you. And you are so grateful and understanding. Nobody understands him like you do.

Of course he does bad things: He's a drug addict who was abandoned by his father. He had a rough life. He can't catch a break now; he's too far down the road. It's your job to ease his pain, to lighten his load, and to perpetually welcome him back into your life with jubilant, open arms whenever he chooses. Wait by the phone, he could be calling. Set your life aside, he could need you to do something for him. Grow up fast, he needs a partner. Ignore your pain, he ain't got the time.

This is so wrong.

You're a child, my love. You're the one who is supposed to be tended to. You're the one whose needs should be put first. No one in your life does this for you. That sucks. And I know it's giving you the impression that your needs don't matter.

They — you — absolutely do.

Unfortunately, you are being raised by emotional midgets. Pariahs. They try to mean well and love you. They do. Yet, they are only going to meet your needs by accident on the path to getting their own crises averted. Your own threshold for drama and stress will defy reason, luring you into dangerous situations more times than you'll want to recount. You'll be tricked by your parents' loveable features. They'll make you laugh, feel loved, and ignore their many shortcomings.

Binary thinking brings comfort: They are good OR bad. It also predicts an emotional boomerang. Just when you're seeing their sickness clearly, they'll swoop in and invite you to feel badly for them or commend their love for you and you'll be lost in their madness again.

Resist it.

Hold your truth.

Know that they, like all of us, have ying and yang; good and bad. Your quest is to decide how much of each you seek and are willing to tolerate in your world. This predicament will rise up over and over again in your relationships. Beyond reason, you'll hang on to the positive traits of someone, continually looking past the grief they deliver to you. You came by this honestly, my dear. Your mom trained you well for a lifetime of toxic, co-dependent relationships.

She placed you in a bind by imbuing you with her own craziness about your father. He continued to be the love her of life, even though he nearly killed the two of you, over and over again. He brought utter joy and devastating fear. She promised him her someday, her forever, regardless of the pain he brought.

You can't reject him or you'll lose her, too. You'll be all alone.

If you push him away, hold him accountable for his actions, they'll live happily ever after and you'll be all alone. It's mind fuckery of the grandest degree.

Unfortunately, you'll also play this story out over and over again in your romantic relationships. You'll hold onto relationships fearing that you'll never survive without them.

Sure, it's delightful that you can see the sunny side of anything; even the humanity in serial killers, but it's a set up for a shit-ton of misery. Sure, everyone has positive characteristics. Clearly, we've all made mistakes that can be forgiven. What you and you alone get to decide is if certain people are healthy enough to take up precious space in your life. If someone had the flu, you wouldn't snuggle up close and get all kissy-face with them. Why? Because you'd rather not get sick, too. The same thing goes for people who are sick emotionally and mentally. You need to keep a safe distance so that you don't wind up in the gutter with them. I'm not recommending that you abandon people who need special care.

I'm simply and passionately advocating for you, Sweet Girl. Cuz no one else is.

The world is not yours to save at your own expense.

You can't fix those who don't want, really want, your help. Distinguishing between those who want your help and those who just say they do is tricky business. You'll get confused over the years, for sure, so go easy on you. There are those out there who will take advantage of your tender heart, fooling you into thinking that you and only you can save them. It's bullshit. They are the only ones who can do that. If they aren't up for that challenge, they'll just draw you into their self-deception and suck you into their madness.

When you catch a glimpse of this, walk away. Gracefully. Lovingly. But clearly and confidently. Your gifts are too precious to squander on those hell bent on swimming in their own misery, their perpetual victimhood.

You are the hero of your story. You cannot be the hero of theirs, not really. Don't confuse heroism with love or you'll live a lonely, lonely life. And you will at times, for sure. These scars run deep. Measure your success in progress not resolution. Total healing will elude you but healing _will_ occur.

You are powerful. You are beautiful. You are worthy of love, real love. You are more than your service to others. You do not need to sacrifice yourself in order to receive love. Because that's not love *anyway. It's manipulation. Just because you learned that model growing up doesn't make it real and true. Let that shit go.*

~ Love, Me

"Let me fall if I must.
The one I will become will catch me." ~ Baal Shem Tov

CHAPTER TWELVE
BARS

Chino, California
1985, Age 14

Today is the day! I got up super early to make sure I look as good as I can. My thighs are huge, my hair is all bumpy, and I hate my clothes. Nothing I can do about it now. I found out a couple of months ago that I could see him if I came to California so I arranged to come with my half-sister and stay with her and her dad for the holidays.

Today is two days after Christmas – his birthday – so our visit needs to be extra special. I made him a gift and packed it in my suitcase so I could give it to him in person. I keep looking at it and realize that it's dumb. It's a shoebox that I decorated with fabric and ribbons to look like a bed. Inside, there's a stuffed animal puppy that I made out of a latch hook kit. I made a blanket and pillow for the puppy, just so he'd be comfortable. It's stupid. What kind of gift is this? It looked cute when I started it. Now that I'm about to bring it to him, I feel like an asshole.

I really just want him to think I look pretty. I want him to be happy to see me. I want to look grown up and beautiful. I want to look sexy. I want him to look at me and think, "Wow!" I want him to not be able to take his eyes off of me. I want him to want me. I want him to realize that he can't live without me. I want him to be compelled to stay in my life and love me.

That's all I want from Daddy.

The ride to the prison seems to take forever. My half-sister drove me down so I could have this visit. I haven't seen him in four years, when I was ten, but we've exchanged photos in the space between so hopefully he'll recognize me. People, especially Mom, tell me that I look just like him.

As we approach the prison, I see the guard towers piercing the blue skies, flanked by intimidating barbed wire fences. Chino is a notorious maximum security prison, much like San Quentin. Daddy's spent time there, too. He even shared stories about Charles Manson and what a wuss he was. I suppose killers aren't all they're cracked up to be.

The way to get to the guard's station confuses us but we finally find the gate where I need to check in. I have the papers that my dad sent to me that prove that I'm on his approved visitors' list.

Unfortunately, it's not enough.

They won't let me in. They won't let me see my dad. He's in there but I can't see him. The only way I can come in is if my parent or guardian brings me in. My brain feels like it's about to explode. One parent is 3,000 miles away. My other parent is inside those walls, behind those bars. *He* could escort me inside. He IS inside. *He's* giving permission for me to go inside.

But *he* doesn't count.

And my half-sister is only 19 and official guardians have to be 21 or over. So she doesn't count either. I've traveled clear across the country, sat in the guard's station, but I can't see my dad. I ask to leave the gift I've made but they refuse to receive or deliver it. I write him an apology note and ask for them to deliver it to him. He's going to be so sad. So angry. Somehow, I messed this up. I didn't see this coming. I didn't get all of the information I needed. I didn't ask the right questions. I didn't map this out well enough.

I screwed up and I'm devastated. I'll pay for this for a good, long time.

~

Oh, Bridget,

What a bullshit movie you're starring in. It's a big, fat, horrible lie. But you can't see it. You're too deep in it. Sometimes when the anger stirs up in you, you can feel the truth piercing the veil of your denial. You have been sold a bill of goods, my dear, tricking you into believing that you are his hero, that it's your job to bring him solace, and that in the process you'll be healed. Here's the truth you keep turning away from:

He's not going to get better and you're going to bleed out trying to help him and attempting to change this story. It's a fool's errand, my dear. If your life was on the big screen, the audience could predict what will happen next. You'll get into relationships with men who you think you can save. You'll predictably fail, over and over again, sending the message to yourself that you are the common denominator so it's your fault. You're not good enough because, if you were, it would all be different. You just need to try harder, be better, stay longer.

Fuck no.

You need to be YOU and walk sooner.

Another truth you keep running from is that you are not his daughter in this sickening narrative. You're his lover.

Next summer he'll draw a card for you for your fifteenth birthday. It will be a detailed image of you in boots with just a man's shirt on, sitting writing "Dear Daddy." And the other picture he drew of a woman in a bra, panties, and thigh high tights. He said he could have named it "Bridget ????" but didn't. Really????

You know at some level that's not normal, to be hit on by your father, but it feels good to be wanted by him, regardless of where the desire emanates from. So you respond provocatively, gratefully, doing his bidding in whatever ways he demands.

After all, he was your first lover.

Whatever you do, you're left empty, always. Empty and soiled. Dripping with filth, emitting the raw stench of incest. Your impulse to vomit from your depths is never realized. The corruption stays with you even when he doesn't. The struggle that defines you right now is that even though you give every part of yourself to him in ways that defy morality let alone good sense, he still walks away. Nothing you ever do or give is enough for him to stay. Or even to show up when he's there. It devastates you. Over and over again. He apologizes and tells you how broken and lost he is. Once again, you are called to heal him.

Until you don't answer anymore.

There will be a day when you will turn and run from this story. You will seek a new narrative, one that is not determined by a destructive and tormented man. With every hurt, you grow in resolve to put yourself first. Just when you think the weight of this will crush you, you'll rise up, casting the load aside.

For now, hear me clearly: You are not this life. You are not this story. You are not your father. You are not his pain. You are not his savior. You are your own beautiful, magical, wise, and wonderful savior. You are powerful, more powerful than you can imagine. These soul-crushing moments will bring you closer to the light and the mysterious glory of this life. If you let them.

Let them.

You're not in prison, my love. You're not bound by anything except the chains your place on yourself. You're still just a child, but you're coming into your own, slowly, steadily. Like a squirrel preparing for winter, you're gathering resources to bring you out of the cold, dark times into the colorful warmth that awaits you on the other side of this. I'll be waiting with open arms and a smile so bright, celebrating your rare perseverance.

~ Love, Me

CHAPTER THIRTEEN

VOICE

力

Townsend, Massachusetts
1986, Age 15

You disgust me.

You don't deserve happiness.

No one this ugly should be loved.

You repulse everyone who sees you. The lumpy, dimply fat that peppers your saggy ass. You thighs are enormous. When your mother was modeling in her twenties she had an 18" waist. You're built like a box.

A fat, hideous box.

Your protruding rib cage that just accentuates your tiny, boyish, useless breasts. Your short waist jacks your already uncool jeans up so high you look like a patronized cartoon character. The clothes you wear just make you look stupid and poor. Nothing looks good on you.

The moles scattered all over you should be used as target practice to put you out of your misery.

After a plastic surgeon refused to remove them, you used scissors to cut two of them off of your skin. They bled for hours but at least they turned colorless when they grew back. Colorless, like your flesh. The boy you love calls you Casper. You've laid under the sunlamp at home and scorched your skin to a blistered mess to alter it. It just returns, more speckled and spotted, every dot a testament to your utter failure.

Your hair is an out-of-control, frizzy, wavy mess. You can't style it like your friends style their hair. They look picture perfect. You look homeless. You're useless. Your chipmunk cheeks and oversized teeth force attention to your old lady lips and narrow mouth. Don't even get me started on your witch nose and chin. Why do you even bother trying to look attractive? No one is fooled by the thick, blue eyeliner and clumpy mascara. Nothing can hide your unique brand of ugliness. Your cheerful disposition and flirty antics just make you more pathetic, like a beacon for your desperation and neediness.

Feel tormented by this inner dialogue? You deserve to feel tearing at the shreds of what is left of your persecuted spirit, piece by miserable piece. Getting dressed for school shouldn't be this hard but you can't even do that right.

You haven't eaten anything in almost two weeks and you're still a fat cow. You walked, ran, rode on your exercise bike in your room, and exercised while doing homework. Nothing. You're still sickening to look at. You did suck on those hard candies to mask the taste of starvation on your tongue. Maybe that reversed your hopeless efforts? I know you. You're so predictable. You'll do what you always do in response: You'll shovel box after box of cookies down your toxic throat and wash it down with vast amounts of milk. You've been binging like this, hiding your stashes of sweets, since you were eight years old. You binge to nourish depths of yourself too dark to access. These days, no one notices your consumption since your parents are too drunk and too busy to notice the missing stock from the pantry. Your record is three boxes of cookies in one sitting. BOXES. Who does that?

You do, you fat piece of undisciplined shit.

Whatever you want in this life you won't get. You'll never amount to anything. Good things don't happen to you. Why would they? You're a whore, a liar, and a thief. At 14, you're used up like a pair of cheap, worn sneakers. No one really cares about you, for good reason. You're a freak. Your friends try to be nice to you, but they see how crazy your life is. They don't say it, but they know you deserve every horrible tragedy that befalls you. You had it coming. You always have it coming.

~

Oh, Bridget,

Siiiiiiiigh.

You really learned from the best, didn't you? That right there is some seriously limiting, painful, and downright abusive talk. You heard pieces of this, no doubt, from one of the people who said you mattered the most to. You can't readily distinguish love from disdain. Care from abuse. Respect from neglect. It's all a jumbled mess in your chaotic mind.

You've sought mirrors to reflect this image right back to you, unfortunately. Even when other mirrors are present, you assume those are the distorted ones and the ugly ones are truth.

When you find yourself on this dark and dangerous island of self-loathing, look across the water and see the land you floated from. The land where your outer beauty and inner magnificence rise above the treetops, casting light over the hills where laughter, joy, and love roam free. That land is truth. Your island is simply the manifestation of your desire for an explanation of why all of this shit has happened to you. The land that explains "why" is far, far away.

I like to call it the Island of Misfit Souls.

You don't belong there. Those who aren't seeking healing but instead do harm to others in their often blind and always misguided state of consciousness. They can only sail away if they choose to, and sadly, most won't. Some, like your parents, will plunge into the island waters, drowning in their guilt-ridden misery.

I wish I could tell you that this self-talk is temporary. It's not. It's going to plague you for the rest of your life. Until it doesn't. I don't know when it'll end. I do know it'll rear its ugly head less and less over time and it won't take you as long to kick that destructive demon to the curb. Self-doubt, your closest companion, will keep inviting you to hold these crazy mean ideas about yourself. Wanna know the clincher? It's mind trickery at its finest.

Deep down in places you haven't yet uncovered, you think that if you admit to being awful you're actually more powerful. If you being fat and ugly is the reason you aren't loved then you can find a pathway to being loved: Lose weight and get prettier. You'll beg for cosmetic surgery to remove your moles. You'll go on diet after diet, chasing skinny like a religion. You hold firm allegiance to the someday that will come that will find you transformed: Thin, pretty, and surrounded by love. You claim all of the power over receiving the love of others, so you hold the pain and the promise. You resist giving anyone else blame for rejecting you 'cause you can't change that. You might be able to change you, though. So you exert Herculean effort toward that mission.

Go easy on you. Whenever and however you can. Look for the mirrors that show you a prettier reflection. More importantly, use that fierce voice you have to hold other people accountable for their shitty, careless treatment of you.

The truth is that no matter how attractive or amazing you are, people are going to be thoughtless dick-muffins.

Over time, after countless injuries to your psyche, you'll find that fierce voice of yours. You'll start seeing where you end and other people begin. You'll figure out that you aren't an extension of others, despite the brainwashing you've endured to the contrary. You'll take your power back. Not the power over the contour of your body, but the shape of your spirit. That's where your true dominion is:

You are powerful over YOU.

Cast the hurtful voices out of your head. They do you no service. They've been a lifelong companion but they must take leave of you. You are the only one who can drive them out by letting kinder, gentler voices in. You are beautiful. Magnificent. Flawed like *everyone else, of course. The cellulite on your thighs doesn't define you. You will be loved, and loved madly, despite every last dimple, spot, bump, and bruise. Just as you love the battered and broken, you will be loved back together. Keep seeking that light, that love, that majesty. Let the other shit go.*

~Love, Me

"The most beautiful people we have known are those
who have known defeat, known suffering,
known struggle, known loss, and have found their
way out of those depths." ~ Elisabeth Kubler-Ross

CHAPTER FOURTEEN
CUFFS

Townsend, Massachusetts
October 31, 1986, Age 15

Twllfwaaap!

Oh my GOD that fucking hurt!

As his hand pulled back from my face I suddenly realize what's happened and why my cheek hurts so damned much.

It's happening again.

I should have seen this coming.

I have been studying people since my life began and this was so predictable. Even a blind squirrel could have seen a car like this coming.

And this is not the first (or the twentieth) time that I've been hit by a man. According to my mom, my dad first beat me bloody when I was just eight weeks old. Just saying those words

126

makes my head pound. Eight weeks old? I've never known a life without a man pounding his rage out on my body.

My mom invites men into her life and her body and I become an ancillary target. Maybe it's more than that? Maybe it's me who is the target and my mom is the ancillary one?

She kept us safe for years. She left my dad behind in California before I turned five and she didn't let my stepfather move in until I was almost thirteen. That was a good stretch. Thanks, Mom.

I'm fifteen now. He's come after me countless times before tonight but tonight is the first time that he actually hit me. Usually he just corners me and rages at me with his words, towering over me with his fists clenched, spitting with fury. How could anyone be so angry at another human being? I don't need to ask this, do I? I know. I've always known.

Can you catch anger, like the flu? I used to watch "The Incredible Hulk" when I was younger and see this mild-mannered Bruce Banner turn into a lethal monster with the flip of a switch.

I've met that monster.

Well, men just like him. And now I'm one of them. I have it inside of me, too. I feel downright volcanic some days. Like I could really spew hot, molten lava over anyone who stirred those demons I hold inside of me. The "anyone" is usually my mom, though. I look just like my dad so the sight of my angry face is enough to frighten her speechless. Like him, I have such deep hatred for her I can hardly contain it some days. I want to punish her for all she's done to me. All the ways she's failed to protect me. For every hit, every penetration, every stinging word, every time I was left alone to fend for myself in this big, ugly world that seems hell bent on destroying me.

I may beat them to it.

My anger comes out as a million "fuck yous" in the things I do. I'm grounded tonight (and for the next two weeks) because I let some friends visit me while I was babysitting for a family in town. They raided the liquor cabinet and I took the fall. My friends can always count on me to take the heat for them so my parents think I do things I just don't do. I do plenty without adding to the pile, trust me. To the outside world, I'm the picture of responsibility and charm. I suppose that's how I landed another babysitting job for tonight. It's Halloween so my mom is convinced that I'm just using the babysitting job as a front so I can go out and party with my friends. I wish.

Besides, as I told her, if that's what's happening all it'll take is a call to the family's house in 20 minutes when I get there and the gig will be up and I'll be in a whole world of trouble. I know I'm reckless but I'm not an idiot. Mom's drinking so she doesn't listen to reason. She wakes up a drama queen; the alcohol just brings out the soap opera addict in her. Next thing you know I'll be in a persistent coma only to wake up and tell her that I'm really her mother and I married the gardener after he divorced my sister who is really my aunt.

But I digress. Sarcasm is my armor and the only thing that keeps me from going completely batshit crazy most days. If I can find the dark humor in something at least I can laugh, even if it's only for a moment. I hold the moment for as long as I can before it slips from my failing grasp.

Mom insisted on waiting with me at the end of our 500-foot driveway for the parents to pick me up for the babysitting job. The sight of my mother, especially when she's wasted, drives me nuts so it's been tense, to say the least. We live in the middle of nowhere so I can't even be distracted by people walking with their kids to trick or treat. That doesn't happen way out here. Nothing like being isolated in Hell.

Stan stumbles down the driveway, beer in hand. He can be such an angry drunk. Sometimes he's silly and playful, but that's rare. When he's like that he's usually groping my mom or coming onto me ("oh, if only I was 20 years younger."). I prefer that nonsense to his violent rages. He threw a lamp at my mom not too long ago. That was fun to listen to. Thankfully, my room is in the basement so I don't have to try to sleep near them.

As soon as his gaze meets mine, he's like a firecracker. He starts calling me names and telling me what a horrible, awful person I am. Stupidly, I try to reason with him, saying that they don't need to wait with me. Reasoning with a raging drunk and a drunk drama whore? I think I'm better at chemistry than people-reading given this embarrassing lapse of judgment. I'm angry, though. Angry that there is such craziness going on in my home and I'm the only one who sees it. I'm the spokesperson and I pay dearly for it. Every single day. Especially today.

Spitting with every word, he reminds me of another night where he threatened to hit me. I stopped him that night with a threat, encompassing what little power I held. He was fighting for custody of his six kids and was accused of being a violent drunk. I had dispelled that in my testimony before the Court years prior. When he had raised his hand to me I protected myself with words: "Want me to be able to testify that you *are* violent?" It stopped him dead in his tracks. I was saved.

Tonight he uses that safety against me.

"Let's see what you can do about it!" as his arm completes the swing toward my waiting face.

~

The symbolism of it being Halloween is not lost on me. Today's the day, nine years ago, that my father murdered my stepmother. Threw her off a bridge, after beating the daylights out of her, I'm sure. Every Halloween, I contemplate how fortunate I am to be alive. Tonight, I just feel sad and tired. I'm not in charge of breaking this pattern of violence. I want to, but I'm still a pawn in my mother's drama. What can I do? I'm fifteen. I'm powerless.

But I'm done. So done. She brings this guy into our lives and he's another abusive, angry drunk. I have to tiptoe in my own house, terrified of his unpredictable temper.

Tonight, alcohol gets the best of him.

Seconds later, the mom I'm babysitting for shows up so I can go to her house to babysit her kids. Sweet relief. My face is pounding, hot, and bright red. My eyes well up with tears, not of sadness, but of recognition. A familiar place returns. Comforted by the darkness in the car that veils my injury, I sit quietly as we make the ten-minute drive to her house. I say little and feel less. Numbness and resolve set in.

Three days later, I'm sitting in a jail cell.

~

Pepperell, Massachusetts
October 31 – November 3, 1986

From my babysitting gig, I call my mom to check in to confirm that I am where I said I was going. She's crying, blubbering some nonsense about how sorry she is for bringing me into this situation....again. She's beyond pathetic. I listen to her but I don't believe her for a second. Her need for a man...and for drama...will trump whatever love she professes for me. It has since jump and today is no different.

She offers empty assurances. She promises me that if I come home that she will leave with me. That we will get away from him. She's nothing if not great at the encore performances. There is a burning in my chest, in my guts, that's propelling me forward. It's spurring me to stand up for myself. To stay clear and strong against the insanity I've been immersed in since birth. I won't tolerate it anymore. That direct hit across my face gave me permission to put an end to this. I feel powerful. I feel hopeful. It's strange to feel this way, to be honest. It's foreign. I'm so much more practiced at feeling desperate and depressed. Lost.

It doesn't last long.

Although I stay in touch with my mom, stay at my best friend's house, go to school on Monday and Tuesday, and stay in that calm, clear head space, my mom doesn't. She fails me like she always does. She succumbs to the power my stepfather has over her, bolstered by the resentment that my half-sister has for me. My mom listens to them. She rises up against me. She demands that I return home, boasting that my stepfather isn't going anywhere either.

I weaken. It's hopeless. There is no change coming. No relief. Just more of the same. Now with me as enemy number one. I relent. I return home on Tuesday. I find the doors locked. What parallel universe have I landed in? We don't lock our doors! I check the windows. The windows are locked. I get the message, loud and clear. A confrontation with my half-sister in the driveway reveals that I am not allowed back in the house until I sign an agreement with my family about my behavior going forward.

I turn and walk away. I was wrong, again. This is not my home.

A few hours later I'm at cheerleading practice at the high school. Two police officers enter the gym. As soon as I see them, I recognize my mother's essence in their movement. This is the drama unfolding at her bequest. They have a warrant for my arrest. I am named a "child in need of services." I am handcuffed and escorted from cheerleading practice. I ride in the back of the squad car. The officer tells me that I've run away from home and I'm out of control. Leaving the place they call "home" is my crime.

I'm brought into the precinct, photographed and fingerprinted. Each finger rolls across the ink and onto the white card on the cold metal table beside it.

Squeeze and roll. Squeeze and roll. Squeeze and roll. Squeeze and roll. Squeeze and roll.

My fingertips stay black. I am officially a criminal. Have I become Daddy? I am alone. They look at me but they don't see me. I am invisible. The officers transporting me to the overnight lock-up a town away try to make gentle conversation. I scream and release cries from deep in my bones. No one can reach me now. The rage and sadness take hold. I am trapped, now in a jail cell with just a tiny little window that looks out into the precinct. It's grey and light in here. I am not. I am darkness. I hear that my best friend's mom wants to see me but my mom has filed a restraining order against her. Even those that want to help me are powerless.

I am darkness. I am alone.

~

Oh, Bridget,

I can feel your anger like a summer storm, cutting a hole in the sky in hopes you change something – anything – about your life. Your vision of how fucked up all of this is drives you mad, almost to the point of insanity, because you're a lonely voice in a cacophony of denial. You know that your mom and stepfather need help, that your sister is an addict in the making, and that your adolescent rebellion is a scapegoat for all the dysfunction swarming around you. Being even slightly sane in a sea of madness is a recipe for drowning.

And you are drowning.

You've seen so much in your fifteen short years, enough to make you into a powder keg of rage and revolt. The question you continue to wrestle with is whether or not you will implode or explode. Will you be the sole casualty or will you leave carnage in your wake? You were born into violence so its scaffolding rests within you. As time passes, you will face critical choices, choices that will define you. Will you follow their sorrowful path or will you pave your own?

I believe in you. I know you have what it takes to be your own person. You were thrown in jail for speaking your truth, for standing up to the abundant injustices in your life. Yeah, you're a royal pain in the ass, but no more so than any other teenager. You're searching for connection and love, acceptance and belonging, but it's not present at home. So you do anything you can to be a part

133

of your friends' lives and the social scene so you can be distracted from the pain that threatens to subdue you. You try to save your friends from themselves, a role you've grown quite accustomed to at home. You're a natural. Your friends — and their parents — love you for it. You have countless pseudo parents out there who see your beauty and want the very best for you.

When you've had your heart broken, you drink like a fish to numb out, to escape the moment. Your parents — well, your mom and stepfather — think you're a horrible person and they treat you with disdain and disregard. I know you don't blame them, really. You're intolerable to be around. But that's okay. It's one of the smartest things you've ever done to protect yourself. If they can't get close, they can't hurt you as easily. Your heart is so tender you'd do just about anything to protect it. Storming around the house like a judgmental, angry bitch certainly keeps anyone from really connecting with you. Well played.

In the years to come, you'll shed this skin. It's a necessary phase, really. You spent your entire childhood taking care of your mother, doing everything you could to fill the treacherous hole in her spirit. When your stepfather moved in a couple of years ago, you were quickly moved out of that role. Instead, she puts on a happy front for him so he has nothing to take care of. He's an angry drunk and he's cruel to her, treatment she is well groomed for.

Some of the only fun you have in that house is when he's in a happy, silly drunk mood and is teasing your mother mercilessly and you join him. It's a beautiful thing, really. You can't get in trouble for releasing the resentment she's burned in you squarely in her face because he's given you permission. You have a free pass and it feels fucking amazing.

Don't confuse this behavior with who you are, though. You are bigger than the torment that stirs in you. You are grander than the way you're acting right now. This time will pass. You will be free of this batshit crazy existence you've come to know. All of this will be in the rearview mirror. Do what you have to do to survive. Just know that everything is temporary. As Grandma Dor always says, "things come to pass, not to stay." This, too, shall pass.

In the meantime, your insight is your blessing and your curse. That which has been seen cannot be unseen, my dear. You see the truth of the insanity of your life so you cannot and will not pretend it away. That marks you as the enemy. You must be silenced; or, better yet, discredited. If they can make you the crazy one, their insanity wins. I'm sorry to be the one to tell you, but the insanity will win many, many times. There are three of them and one of you and they are wedded to the story that serves their disease.

Your mission, sweet girl, is one of survival. You'll do plenty of damage to yourself along the way, wandering in the dark in search of the light. Do me a favor? Forgive yourself. Wake up in the morning forgiving yourself and go to sleep at night full of loving forgiveness for whatever you did to make it another day. Make no mistake: I'm not giving you a free pass to be a jerkbutt.

Simply live by this adage: Do no harm, but take no shit.

You are wise. You are destined for greatness. Your voice is rising to the surface, even though you were punished for it this time. You'll get knocked down plenty of times, trust me. But you'll get up more times than you fall. That voice of yours won't quit. It gets stronger over time, despite how weak you sometimes feel. And, oh how weak you feel, Love. I know you think that no one is in your corner. Think again.

See the angels in your midst. The lawyer whose face melted when he saw you curled up in the corner of your jail cell, like a dog beaten into submission. The foster parents who treated you like a human being hungry for respect. Mr. Steimel, your guidance counselor, who continues to see through the bullshit exterior you paint over your anguished spirit. He knows. He understands. Your English teacher, Mrs. Margolis sees your pain and your potential. They all want to help, but they are rendered powerless.

You? You are powerful.

You will rise up.

Rise up.

~ Love, Me

"I no longer look to my abusers with any expectation-
of remorse, or apology or restitution or restoration or
relationship. I'm at peace, accepting that they won't and can't
help me out of the mess they created.
But, I'm the best qualified for that job anyway and I'm happy
with the job I'm doing." ~ Christina Enevoldsen

CHAPTER FIFTEEN
GOODBYE

Fitchburg, Massachusetts
October, 1987, Age 16

"I couldn't even kill myself right."

Everything is still so hazy. My hospital room is bright, but it's like there is smoke in the room. The doctor's face is cloudy. He's talking to me, asking me questions. If I regret the overdose I took last week, the one that landed me in the intensive care unit until today? The one that had me drinking liquid coal in the emergency room. The one that consisted of enough of my mom's epilepsy medication to kill four grown men. Plus the nasty beer. And the aspirin.

My mistake was the aspirin. The doctor said it might have been enough to thin my blood so that the other poison was less effective. Plus, I crawled upstairs from my room and my parents found me early in the morning on their way to their paper delivery routes. Conflicted about my decision, I'd gone up to get more beer...or to be found...I still couldn't decide from the stairs. When I reached the top of the stairs, I made quite a racket, knocking over a chair and crashing to the ground. That should wake them. They'll find me. They'll see me in this altered state and bring me to the hospital. It'll make them see how messed up we all are, they'll get us help. They'll stop drinking. They'll break this cycle. They'll save me.

They slept right through it.

The drugs really kicked in by the time they got up for work. Again, I'm indecisive. I mumble that I'm sleepy. My mom drags me down the stairs to bed to rest. Collapsing onto my bed, the world spins. I've consumed a gallon bottle of wine in under five minutes and I've never felt this drunk. This is what dying feels like. I'm slipping away from this world. All its pain will soon be behind me. I'll leave a corpse behind. My mom will find my lifeless body here when she tries to wake me for school in a few hours. Dead. I'll be dead. Isn't that what I wanted?

As my mother approaches my bedroom door to leave, a small voice rises up in my belly. I've met that voice before; she's scared now. She doesn't want to die. She just wants someone to see her. To see the excruciating pain in her eyes. To hold her and tell her that she's loved. That she matters. That she doesn't deserve to be abused. That she hasn't been forgotten.

The little voice moans. Her mom is still leaving. Her moan grows louder. What is her moan saying? "No." It's just saying, "no." Just one little, insignificant word. That's all she can make her weakened body sound out. Her mother turns around. "No," just a little louder this time. This whole time, she's been clutching the empty Dilantin bottle, the pills dissolved into her bloodstream by now, turning her brain to mush.

"Noooooo." The little word gets bigger, longer, louder.

I'm not in my body anymore. I can't feel pain, just a distant heaviness. A lowering of my body onto the floor where I can't rise from.

My mom sees the bottle fall out of my fist. She calls out to my stepfather. She needs help. I can't move on my own. My body is lifeless. My mind is barely hanging on to the moment.

Somehow, I'm in the car. My mom is asking me questions.

"I drank. I'm drunk." I'm lying but I don't know why.

Now I'm on a bed in the emergency room, looking up at lights so bright they burn my eyes. The nurse asks me questions. I slur, I stumble. I tell her about the drugs I took. My mom is there but I can't see her face. They hand me something to drink. It's black and thick. The nurse says it's charcoal to soak up the poison.

Poison.

Poison kills. I'm alive. I can't decide if this upsets me. I just know I like this numbness more than anything I've felt in a long time.

~

Dear Bridget,

You're so close. So close to freedom. So close to getting out of the box you're trapped in. You don't need to put yourself in another box to do it. Don't give up, please, Baby. I know you feel so alone, so lonely, so full of emptiness, so desperate to find something safe to hold onto. Your best friend, Tanya, refers to you as a candle in the wind, a fitting Elton John reference.

That's you. Adrift in a sea of monsters.

You want to live, but not like this. I know deep down you don't want to die. You just want someone to care that you might. If you could be assured to come back, you'd die just to see who would come to your funeral and how devastated they'd be. Would your dad be devastated? Would he vow to change his ways? Would your friends see the depth of your pain and pledge to see the sorrow beneath your smile? Would your parents wake up and stop seeing you as the problem?

Some of those things might happen, but it would be too late. Too late for you to get any satisfaction or calm from any of it. You'd be dead. There's no coming back from dead. You'll find that now you're just seen as a fragile basket case which really didn't make anything better. If anything, it made it worse at home. Now you really are the broken one, the identified patient. They're going to redouble their efforts to fix you, blind to the real issues. Sure, you need healing, but it's like treating an injury that you promptly assault with a baseball bat. Without fixing the people around you, the ones responsible for your care, you're stuck in the same shit storm with a pocket umbrella. In your time at the psych hospital, you figured out the root of your anger which was a start, but it's going to be another couple of years before any real works gets done in that noggin of yours. As long as you live in that house, you're in survival mode.

My advice?

Give fewer fucks. Don't fight the power. Realize that you can't change a damn thing so don't tire yourself trying. You're off to college in a matter of months; and you don't know this yet, but you'll fall in love right after graduation with a man who wants nothing more than to love you for the rest of his life. You won't let him, of course, but he'll be your saving grace for a year, whisking you out of your house a couple of months earlier than expected and take your sweet ass all the way to Florida. That should give you a bit of a buffer to start mending yourself.

You'll fall apart again when you leave his safe haven and return to the war zone, but you're you so you'll keep getting back up. You'll continue to look for every silver lining possible. You'll go blind, literally, just to open your eyes to more truth about the challenges you face getting to peace in your world. The doctors won't fix you – they give up and define you as legally blind. You'll fix you. In true Bridget fashion, you'll hear that diagnosis relegating you to a lifelong handicap and say, "screw that!" As quickly as your sight left you, it will return. The doctors will be perplexed, trying to make sense of this spontaneous healing of an undefined condition. Like I keep telling you, you are fierce. You don't yet know your own strength, but you will. These are tests and testimonies to your incurable resilience.

You are powerful. Hold onto that when the storms come, knowing that you are more formidable than any challenge you face.

~ Love, Me

BACKSTORY FOUR
DESPERATELY SEEKING

"And once the storm is, you won't remember how you made it through, how you managed to survive. You won't even be sure, in fact, whether the storm is really over. But one thing is certain. When you come out of the storm you won't be the same person who walked in." ~ Haruki Murakami

~

~ Fighting For Scraps ~

My father spent my childhood in and out of jail. The only times I ever heard from him was when he was in jail. When he wasn't in jail, he was doing things that were going to land him there: Doing drugs, manufacturing drugs (usually meth), building bombs and firearms, and simply blowing off (thankfully not *up*) his parole officer.

He was super attentive when he was behind bars. He sent letters and requested packages. He called collect often, even buying me an answering machine so he could yell his next call time over the voice of the operator when it picked up. These were the days before cell phones, texting, or even pagers. Letters and phone calls were the only mode of communication, both fraught with delays and misfires.

I also had a life that didn't have him in the center of it. I was a solid student involved in student government, cheerleading, and had a strong group of friends. During most of high school, my friends thought my father was dead. Why? Because I told them that he was. It seemed easier than telling them that he left me over and over again. Death he couldn't help. Leaving me? That he chose to do.

My father's departures were agony, but his returns were equally tormenting. What would be enough to keep him around this time? What could I do or say or give to draw him in and make him want to stick around? Every phone call could be the last, and I knew that. I obsessed over what I would say to him, presents I could make and send, how dutifully I could follow his directives. I read his poetry over and over again, searching for clues to his recovery and healing. I wanted to live by the phone so that he'd know that he could count on me.

He made me feel so loved and so special when he called and wrote. I was his reason for living. His miraculous munchkin. A bright light in a dark world. I had to live up to all of that, and make him feel loved, wanted, and accepted. I had to excuse every abandonment, fearing that making him feel guilty would push him away. No matter how inappropriate he was, I felt compelled to giggle and let it ride.

I knew other parents weren't like him so I kept so much of him a secret. I told one friend in elementary school about him, his drug use and jail time, and my mom's marijuana habit. When her mother found out, she called me a slut and told me I wasn't welcome in their home anymore. I felt so ashamed of them but I couldn't let him know that or he'd have one more reason to run away. His absences were downright excruciating. Waiting for a someday that might never arrive was nerve-wracking and left me with a deep anxiety about the unknown. I wanted nothing more than to be able to count on his affections, to know that he was safe and healthy, to feel proud of my parents and their life choices. I felt their every lapse as though it was my own.

To put it in black and white, my mom and I left California for Massachusetts a year after my last unsupervised visit with my dad. I wouldn't see him again until I was almost 9. I saw him when he surprised me with a short visit when I was 10. We stopped to see him and his new wife in North Dakota during our cross-country road trip when I was 11. My attempted visit that Christmas when I was 14, had it succeeded, would have been the next time I would have seen him, the fourth time since I was 3.

Despite my deep longings otherwise, I would see him one more time when I was 17.

~ Eating the Crazy ~

The only thing I felt I could remotely control was food and the shape of my body.

It was something I could focus on, an aspect I could attempt to control. It gave me hope that I could be loved, happy, connected, wanted. I tried self-tanning and ended up with severe burns. Anything to be different, yet the same. Unlike myself yet like those I envied. I couldn't get skinny enough. I only felt moderately attractive for minutes at a time. The feeling was always fleeting and reliant on the approval of others. One sideways glance and I was gross again. My self-esteem hung in a precarious balance.

I would sell my soul for flattering attention. A glimpse into the experience of feeling love, especially from a man, was my drug.

My diet was deplorable. Fruit rotted on the counter. There was nothing edible in the fridge, most of it was growing mold. Cookies, safe in the plastic, were safe. Pasta, if I cooked it myself, was edible. It still perplexes me how my struggle was invisible to my mom. It was all part of my distance from the family, my invisibility.

My bedroom was in the dark, smelly basement. No windows. No doors to the outside. Dampness. Flooding under the elevated floor. Spiders. Spiders that would bite me on my legs, under my covers as I slept. Crawl on my pillows. My face.

It mirrored my perception of what I deserved.

And then it didn't.

~ Standing Up To the Crazy ~

Of all of the stories contained in this book, the story of my "running away" is the only one that I told with humor and sarcasm. By this point, I could see how insane my life had become and my rage at that boosted my confidence to comment on it. I would gloss over the emotion of it and instead focus on the lighter moments. Like when I removed my bobby pins from my hair and slid them to the inmate in the cell next to mine so he could attempt to pick the lock on his jail cell. If he succeeded, at least I could feel like I helped someone and actually deserved being treated like a criminal.

The players in this telenovela each brought me a different view of it:

The judge who almost sent me to juvenile hall could only see my rage and disrespect.

The public defender saw that I was a good kid with a tender heart who needed help and support, not punishment.

The foster parents I was sent to live with gave me care, concern, and a boatload of empathy.

My parents took responsibility for nothing, putting the blame for it all squarely on my "out-of-control-teen" shoulders.

No one called my parents out on their alcoholism, emotional and physical abuse, and mental illness.

When I returned home, I was numb, resolved. I committed to surviving my life there, making as few waves as possible, staying as far away from them as possible. I was stoic and resigned. I was smart enough to know that I wasn't safe and would never be supported or protected. That just as easily as I was arrested and sent away this time, I'd be in juvenile detention the next time in no time flat.

I couldn't give them that satisfaction.

A year later, I offered myself up on a cross. Or a gurney, to be more accurate.

~ Choking Back the Crazy ~

When I swallowed those pills, I was swallowing more pain that a heart should bear.

It was my third, and final, suicide attempt. I was in eleventh grade, planning to graduate in the spring a year early. Anything to break free of the life I was smothered by. I'd tried to kill myself in seventh and eighth grades, as well. I took my mother's epilepsy medication in seventh grade but there weren't enough left in the bottle to do anything but give me a hangover. In eighth grade, my guidance counselor heard about it through a friend of mine so he called my mother. She was spitting mad at me. I'd used the expensive pain killers we had for one of our cats. She couldn't believe I'd "wasted" them like that. I'll never forget the look on the counselor's face, a look that validated for me that I was, indeed, living in madness.

I find it darkly amusing that even given her concern about my "wastefulness," she never hid any medications after that. Her daughter had overdosed and she still left deadly medications in a bottom drawer in our kitchen amongst the vitamins that I took daily. What an invitation.

I'm not sure that I ever wanted to die, exactly. I just wanted the pain to stop. I wanted someone, most especially my dad, to see me and my pain; to recognize my writhing and put an end to it. It was my cry for help. I was on fire and the only way out of that pain was put out the flames by ending my life.

It was my greatest act of rebellion paired with my biggest act of loyalty.

Both of my parents said that the only reason they pressed on was because of me. They would have given up already if it wasn't for me. It was such a bind. If I failed in any way, would they perish? I could "kill" my own parents if I wasn't careful. And suicide was a reasonable option. A legitimate way out. My little rebellion.

It was also a form of loyalty. They slept with their depression all of their adult lives. Succumbing to my own with such finality, doing what they hadn't yet been bold enough to do, let my shiny apple-self fall close to the base of their dangerous trees.

This last attempt, when I was 16, was spurred on by a few things.

Just a few months before, my father had missed yet another birthday of mine. My sweet sixteen. I felt incredibly lonely and dismissed. Invisible. Weeks later I had consensual sex for the first time. I chose to sleep with the boy I'd loved for years. He was an addict so it was no wonder how desperately I loved him, but he had no capacity to love me back. He continually chose other girls over me. I took this to mean that I wasn't a girl boys took seriously. I wasn't a girl boys made their girlfriend. I was good for sex and comfort but not respect. Love maybe, but forbidden, hidden love.

My inner filth seeped through my pores somehow, destining me for perpetual abandonment.

I knew I had to make a shift, change my life somehow. A few weeks into the start of my junior year in high school I realized that I could graduate that same year if I gave up my study hall and did a few extra projects to earn the remaining credits. This would get me out of high school, out of my house, a year early. God, that sounded so good.

Some thought that taking on this extra pressure is what drove me to suicide. They couldn't see that graduation just wasn't coming soon enough.

I overdosed the night that I'd hosted one of those catalog parties at a local lingerie shop for my friends, only my friends didn't show up.

And, no, it's not lost on me that I was sixteen and having a party at a lingerie shop.

I sat there for an hour with the owners of the shop, alone. I finally left and went home, alone. My friends had good reasons for not coming, but I didn't care. Together, they'd left me alone. No one chose me.

I let all of their calls go to my answering machine. I pushed them all away and swallowed the pills instead.

When I got out of intensive care and was questioned by the hospital psychiatrist, they concluded that I was still a danger to myself. I was taken by ambulance, strapped down, to an inpatient facility about 45 minutes away where I stayed for a few weeks.

They told me that I intellectualized things. That I needed to feel more things. That I needed to face my pain. When that unwrapped my anger, I spent time in a locked, padded room. Oh, how I loved the confined space. Not. My father sent me an apologetic letter, wondering if he landed me there. Oh, Daddy. I can't make you feel better right now.

My mom came to the hospital for a "family" session but took no accountability for what was making me sick in the house. I was living in emotional asbestos yet they sent me back in to scrape the ceiling and still expected me to recover.

When they released me, I was sent to another shrink. I attended just to comply. Nothing was accomplished. I didn't trust him not to see me as the problem. So I sat there, feeling alone.

Feeling all alone in the world was home to me.

I'll leave you with some poetry my father sent to me when I was little, poetry I poured over again and again in his absences, searching for clues on how to help him, heal him, save him, save myself.

In this mission, I failed. Again and again and again. Yet, the answers were right in front of me all along.

I couldn't.

How We Rise Up From Our Pain

Untitled (1980)
By Jerry Cannon (aka, Daddy)

"Scared, afraid, terrified, trembling.
Am wondering of what I am most afraid.
The cold, dark, uncertainty of death or
The lonely, painful, sadness of life.

I fear both.

But the pain of life grows worse
And the fear of death grows smaller.
With the passing of each lonely minute
I grow weak, Lord save me. Lord love me.

I want to live!
I need someone to care.
I need someone to touch me, hold me, care for me, comfort
me, and give me a few moments' rest.

From all the sadness and loneliness.
From all the pain and fear.
But my wants and needs matter little.

All that matters is to escape.
Escape from this pain.
This damned burning from within that threatens to crush my
soul and destroy my sanity.

Escape, escape. Only one thought: Escape.
Even if I have to escape to the darkest pits of Hell."

CHAPTER SIXTEEN

ENOUGH

力

Amherst, Massachusetts
January 1990, Age 18

I'm such a fool.

I believed in him. Again. I thought he had changed. Again. I thought he loved me enough to turn things around. For once.

Never.

Yet, maybe I knew all along. Always.

Awaiting release from another prison term, he insisted on sending me the considerable funds off his prison bank account because he didn't trust the system to return them to him after he was paroled.

I warned him. I did. I told him what I'd do if he screwed up again. I'd keep all of the money. I'd both punish and protect him from using it to get high. I pleaded with him to not give me that power over him. He'd screw up and I'd be in control.

Never hand an angry person the keys to the castle; you'll end up in the moat, with the dragons.

Underneath it all, I held rage fueled by years of broken promises and repeated abandonment. I seethed while trying to appease myself, waiting for a miracle. A corner turned. A new day. I'm so tired yet the anger stirs inside of me, giving me energy. Energy to do what has been gnawing at me for years: To send my rage in his direction. My mother and stepfather and my reflection in the mirror have absorbed it for so long. I've protected him from it always.

This was the final straw. I should have seen it coming, but only hindsight is 20/20. This was blurry at best.

I called his girlfriend yesterday to arrange to send her some money for phone bills and care packages she'd sent while he was incarcerated. He'd insisted.

I wasn't prepared for what she shared.

"Have you spoken with him? The bastard is up in the hills getting high. I haven't heard from him in days."

Out of prison? For days? Getting high?

Oh, I'd heard from him. The day before on a collect call. Supposedly from jail. He wasn't getting out for another week. He'd call when he got out.

Liar liar, pants on fire.

He'd played me for a fool for the last time. Only eighteen, I'd had enough deception and games to last forever.

He'd lied to buy himself time to relapse, to go off the grid, to hide from me.

Now he'd pay.

His girlfriend served as my messenger. No money for you, Daddy. Say goodbye to your daughter and your bank account together, permanently. Oh, and your girlfriend gets double the money you requested just for having to deal with you.

My dorm room phone rings. The room seems to grow suddenly quiet, the ringer amplified. Every cell in my body starts to quiver with anticipation. I've been walking slowly toward this moment for my entire life but I fear I'm not ready. I call on rage as my fearless companion, shaking as I take the receiver in my hand and mutter, "hello?"

It's him. Not an operator announcing a collect call. Just him. From his hello I grasp two immediate truths: He's furious and he's high on heroin. I know his heroin voice. It floats in the air with no clear pattern or connectedness. The rage seeps through the wires as he speaks in a low, measured tone. I can think of nothing else other than fiercely defending my newly-found courage. I stand up to him. I hold the line. I refuse to return his money despite his demands. He was warned. This time, for the first time in my life, I hold the power.

Something about this power intoxicates me, frees me to unleash every ounce of pain held for so long. I scream out from the depths of my broken soul and I heave my rage directly at him. I tell him all of the pains I remember, and all those told to me by him and my mom. Like an impassioned prosecutor, I hold him accountable for every cut, bruise, scar, and tear. I leave nothing out. Nothing.

Mount Vesuvius looks tame compared to my verbal lava.

It burns as it flies out of my mouth, searing my throat and stinging my tongue. My own words hurt me, staking claim on the mountain of pain I'd been building for so long. As I own these words, I make them real, irrefutable, and forever pinned to my life. I hurl them at him with such vengeance that I feel possessed. My body in tremors, I pace around my room, the receiver in my left hand, the base in my right. Tethered to the cord, I make figure eights, hoping to unravel the thoughts and feelings that haunted me.

His silence is deafening. As the silence grows in the space between us, I rage on and on, unapologetically emptying myself into it. I've never even raised my voice to him, rarely showing any form of displeasure, forever fearful that I'd scare him away. That he'd leave and never return.

Today, I'm ready. I'm prepared for his permanent departure. It's me or him. Him or me. I can't survive another one of his relapses. I can't move past another disappearance. And I can't hold this pain inside another second. I have to make it his. I have to deliver it to him on a bloody silver platter.

I run out of words, repeating myself has worn me out. In the pause, he speaks. The pause is my downfall.

"The reason I kept leaving you is because I couldn't stand to be around you for very long. You are such a little bitch. You'd better watch your back because you're going to get what's coming to you, you fucking cunt."

SMASH.

The phone breaks into pieces against the brick wall and falls to the floor.

I follow.

The connection severs. Forever.

~

Bridget,

I couldn't be prouder of you. The mantras you have hanging on your wall provide your roadmap and life preserver: "The only way out is through" and "God gives His most to His best players."

You got this. I'd be a liar if I told you this was going to be easy. You're going to want to throw in the towel many times, but you won't, not for long anyway.

Knowing you like I do, I know you're feeling a mixture of dread, regret, and relief right now. You have a violent criminal who threatened your life. Each day you find yourself looking around for him, wondering when he's going to bring his promised wrath down upon you. This will last a long time, but I promise it'll fade eventually, taking up less and less space in your brain.

You wonder if you made the right call, pushing your dad out of your life, probably for good. You knew he was hurting you and you stood your ground, finally handing him all the hurt you were holding in for so many years. It was brutal.

You'll regret this conversation for decades, not because you didn't have the right to behave as you did. No, Baby. You'll regret it because the ball of anger you developed around was what exploded that day. Your very core came barreling out and you stepped out of its way so it could be purged. It was an ugly piece of your tortured soul.

With each passing year, you become more of who you were meant to be. The gentle, calm, joyful, grateful, compassionate spirit that fought to survive. The regret you will harbor emanates from how unfamiliar that rage feels. You'll regret the long possession of your soul that ended that day. You'll work tirelessly to buff out the scratches and burns left behind by all of that anger, and work to heal the places that stir up those desperate feelings. Sometimes you'll be successful; sometimes you'll make a sincere mess of things. It's okay. Just keep trying to do better. Learn from your mistakes. Know that rage like that leaves scars on the giver as much or more than the receiver.

You had to drive him out of your life. You had to do it in grand fashion or it would never have stuck. You had to give a voice to your pain, to begin the healing process. You don't know it now, but this was your last contact with your father. He will die five years later, unbeknownst to you. You'll find out a month later by doing what you do best: searching for him.

It'll be too late.

You won't be able to undo this. You will always know that the last three words your father ever said to you are: "You fucking cunt." This will unravel you. You'll draw so many lessons from this experience, mostly constructive ones.

You'll try to get a do-over of sorts through your marriage. You'll marry a man who shares his birthday, and his penchant for cruelty. When he's mad at you, he'll sling those same three words at you time and time again, knowing their symbolism and their power to dismantle you. You will fear him and succumb to his rage for a decade before you manage to walk away. But you will walk away. It'll be a calculated departure. Swift, deliberate, and unequivocal. Drama will surround it, but your energy will be different than when you bid your dad farewell. You will stand more clearly, more calmly, and with far more grace — amazing grace — which is a better reflection of your true, perpetually-healing essence.

Casting your father out of your life was an act of both defiance and brilliance. When you recount this story to others you will begin to see how strong you are and what you are capable of when you set your mind to it. You'll begin to see that you were victimized but you need not be the victim. With practice, you'll learn how to wield your power with honor, coming from love even when it seems undeserved. You are love so you will carry this with you. When you find yourself responding intensely, know that you are being triggered, brought back to a powerless place you once occupied. Don't get confused for long: You are powerful. Own that power and treat it with respect. When others seek to dominate you, recognize their own feelings of powerlessness. Yours is not a power that demands to be dominion over others; yours is power from within.

Hang tough.

~ Love, Me

BACKSTORY FIVE

FINIT

"It takes a great deal of bravery
to stand up to our enemies, but just as much
to stand up to our friends." ~ J. K. Rowling

~

Blowing my dad out of the water like I did sure wasn't smart but it sure was brave.

Sounds like the story of my life. Step by step, I was laying the groundwork for my inner badass.

Standing up to our parents poses great difficulty for most of us, but is often our passage into adulthood. It was my passage into health and set me on my path to recovery. I had to have distance or I would have drowned in all of it. Months later I would refuse to return home again where my mom and stepfather lived because of his rage at me, at her, and her refusal to protect me or herself. I was growing intolerant of victims, including myself.

This goodbye was, by far, the hardest thing I ever did. And the best.

In my case, this man was larger than life. He was the villain and the hero. My abuser and my lover. My greatest hope and my deepest fear. Exorcising him out of my life ripped me in two, right down the boundary line between what I hoped for and what I reconciled to be truth. I let out every ounce of rage I ever bottled up inside of myself to make sure that I left nothing unsaid. If I was going to rise up I was going to do it with passion. And permanence.

None of it was an act. I experienced those emotions with such power and intensity it scared the shit out of me. I was so possessed with anger my voice sounded almost demonic. He surely didn't recognize me, though I'm sure the family resemblance was striking.

When my dorm director found out about the conversation and his violent history, I was implored to go into some form of a residential protection program so that he couldn't find me.

He was a murderer. An angry one. And I was now a target.

With my burgeoning rebellion, I decided that I wouldn't live in fear, that I wouldn't live my life looking over my shoulder. I knew that if he wanted to find me he would, name change or not. I embraced the danger as a testimony to my bravery and lived my life.

A life devoid of a father, and the hope of a life itself.

A life that mourned that last conversation, one that ended in my worst fears realized: That he had blamed all of his absences on my failings as a daughter. That he thought I was a fucking cunt who deserved to die.

He died from liver failure 5 ½ years later at the age of 45. The work that began that frigid night in that little dorm room to pick up the tiny pieces of myself and fasten them back together started all over again when I learned, by phone, of his death. His "expiration." And my absence from his end. Our story's revised, healing end.

As it so happened, this was our final farewell. Our last words spoken. Burning, bitter, seething, heart-rending words. His were, "You'd better watch your back because you're going to get what's coming to you, you fucking cunt."

~

Alexandria, Virginia
1998, Age 26

"You're such a fucking cunt!"

My boyfriend is standing over me as I'm huddled in fetal position in the corner of my luxury fourth-floor apartment. After getting my master's degree, I've got a good job with a salary bigger than my mother ever made in her entire working career. I'm doing so well, on a path to bigger and better things. Realizing my full potential.

How did I get here?

I'm crying, begging for him to stop. He won't stop. He's furious.

I started a conversation about how I didn't feel loved by him. I told him I wanted to feel closer to him. I wanted to feel more attractive to him. Our sex life was lacking. I wanted to feel more connected to him. He always seemed so angry at me. I said that. I shouldn't have said that. He doesn't like it when I say that.

How did I get here?

~

This was only two short years after my father's death. My wounds raw, this felt like I was bathing in acid. This boyfriend who later asked me to marry him was ripping me into tiny shreds. This man who shared my father's birthday.

The cruelty.

The power.

The pain.

Enduring, I marched on. This time, it only took me a decade to break free of our bond. To start over. To choose light, my light. To stand in contrast to the models from which I sprung. To risk everything to gain myself.

I changed forever that night when I was eighteen and struggling to find a reason to live and the strength to send my primary abuser into the wind.

I've changed a little every day since.

Becoming known as a fucking cunt again returned me to the cage I'd resigned my prior life to.

Slowly, painfully, and at great cost, my life as a cage rattler began to unfold.

CHAPTER SEVENTEEN

MEANING

"History, despite its wrenching pain,
cannot be unlived, but if faced with courage,
need not be lived again." Maya Angelou

~

Sigh.

I didn't plan to write this book until many years from now. A year in the distant future when my daughters would be old enough to properly digest its content. A time when my career wouldn't be my family's mainstay, lessening the risk of being so candid and revealing. A time when standing boldly in the light would be easier.

I'm not known for taking the easy path so why start now?

The photo of that baby was my doing and my undoing.

Aside from forgiveness, trust has been my greatest stumbling block. When you've been abused, trust takes on such perverse meaning. You're often forced out of necessity to trust those who have violated you, building your life on quicksand.

In opening the door to these transformative experiences in my private life, I placed my trust in you, an act that scared the shit out of me. My ex-husband knew about these events in a cold, general manner, and he threw them at me whenever I was hurt by something he did, painting me as a damaged basket case. I have countless emails, notes, and court transcripts in which he sold me as psychotic, broken beyond repair because of my past.

It's like he reached into my soul, grabbed it in his angry fist, squeezing and twisting it unrelentingly. Being seen as forever crazy and splintered remains my greatest fear.

Yet, I offered that potential up on a silver platter to a world of strangers.

Go big or go home, B.

In some sense, it's really all about trusting in *myself*. Trusting that I can handle whatever life throws at me. Whatever you throw at me. Whatever *anyone* throws at me. That I can take the punches and keep standing; or, at least keep getting back up. That I will be courageous and resilient, even though I feel pain.

Damn straight I will.

I am not these stories. I am not my abuse. Yet, they are a part of me, always. Woven together, they are the mosaic of my life. What gives my life the color, brilliance, and magic is what I've done with my stories, for bad and for good. Narrative therapy tells us that the meaning we make of our life originates in the stories we tell about our life, in the details and in the shading. When I let the darkness reign, I am smaller for it. When I let the light dominate, I am better for it.
And you can be, too.

I came to realize that
life never stops
bringing you pain no matter
how smart or strong
you become.
Your job in life
is to not let it break you.

What happens to us does not define us. What we do with what happens to us *does*. The world is abundant with those examples if we are willing to see things through that lens. People lose limbs in tragic, horrific acts of terror and emerge as heroes, warriors of the light. Others lose those very same limbs in parallel tragedies and become angry, isolated, examples of self-destruction. Both were entitled to anger, rage, resentment, and sadness. The choice was in how those emotions dominated their respective existences. Both could end up on a rooftop.

One would be singing.

One would be shooting.

I choose to sing.

Armed with this book, I set out on this journey to give a voice to those who have forgotten their voice.

To offer the memory of a child long forgotten: Me.

Not only did the world forget her, but I forgot her, too. Over the years, I've shared my trauma resume...a laundry list of events I experienced with no real details or emotions tied to them...to those interested in hearing it.

One thing that was lacking was *me*.

Imagine that? In documenting my history I left my own experience out of it. I never put myself behind my own eyes to see what it was like to live in and through those things. To use my five senses to really *be* in those moments again. Yet, I tied myself to the abuse and the abusers by holding onto my pain and scars and recounting my "list."

A number of years ago I was shaken free from this pattern of defining myself by my abuse when I considered that the reason

I kept sharing my list was to validate my experience. That without me sharing it, it would disappear. No one had been held accountable. There were no court records to review. No one in jail for their crimes.

My experience would disappear with my silence.

Yet, simultaneously, I tormented myself over and over with that list of violations, tying me close to my abusers, some crazy sort of victim-perpetrator loyalty pact. Remembering to forget and forgetting to remember. What a fucked up mess I was. What a journey this has been.

~ Pulling It All Together ~

I'm in my mid-forties as I write this so it's clear that I've done a whole lot of living since the time of that last story. Why did I stop *there*? It marked a shift in my consciousness, a moment in which I took the power of my life into my own hands and that changed everything.

I chose life, at whatever the cost. I chose freedom from a toxic relationship, whatever the pain. I chose compassion, even though it came in dribs and drabs. I healed myself through choice, by taking control, finally, over a life that had never been mine. I took control where I could: Over my thoughts, feelings, and behaviors. I set myself on a path of self-discovery, one that would be marked by crushing failures and glorious triumphs. A lifetime of little landslides.

There were great lessons in my pain, if I paused thoughtfully and long enough to understand and appreciate them. Seeing how they served me somehow lessened the burn, allowing me to witness a higher purpose in my journey. Now it's my turn to do the same for you through my words, my stories, my perspectives, and my sought-after advice. I talk with people about their problems and stressors every day and I know some part of them questions the depth of my empathy.

This book should leave no question.

I'm sending prayers on high that I didn't cause pain to anyone connected with this book by sharing all of these barbaric details. I am clear that the people depicted in this book had both positive and negative qualities. That they did both good and bad things. They were perfectly imperfect. They were flawed. Ugly and beautiful. Full of joy and burdened with despair.

I loved my parents. I really did. I got to tell two of the three of them that before they died. I was able to release our pasts as best I could before they moved on. In the years since their respective passings, I've had plenty of opportunities to reconcile our relationships, studying them like my life depends on it.

Because it *does*. When I carry my pain from moment to moment, I slowly die inside.

I continue to celebrate the abundant gifts they gave to me. All three of my parents were funny as hell and made my cheeks hurt sometimes laughing at their antics. They were all creative geniuses in their own right, making me gifts big and small, all precious.

They were generous to a fault. My father literally gave a stranger the shirt off of his back. He was a masterful poet and artist with a wicked sense of humor.

My mother somehow managed being a single mom in a time that this wasn't the norm and made sure that I attended college so that I could make my life better. She taught me powerful lessons about life, love, and humanity. She instilled in me a quirky sense that there would always be enough money and resources for my needs which made me feel safer in the world.

My stepfather taught me about football, wrestling, woodworking, and card games. He was silly and spirited and showed devotion to his six children, countless grandchildren, and great grandchildren. I got to speak about the ups and downs of our complicated relationship at his funeral, capturing laughs by paying tribute to his precocious, adventurous side.

My parents were unique and wonderful and beautiful and gifted. My parents were burdened and sad and scarred and struggling.

The hardest truth to swallow: They loved me.

They did so pretty poorly for chunks of time, but they did. I knew that then and I know that now. It doesn't lessen the pain, but it offers a clarity about the balance of life, of our stories, of the many layers inherent in our human experience.

I'm not going to pull punches. These stories were pretty horrific. I refuse to disrespect the stories – and you – by glossing over that fact. I recognize that you have your own stories, some more or less disturbing than these, that brought you to a crossroads, whether you recognized it or not. You've been given the chance over and over again to take those experiences and have them make you bitter or better.

When the residue of the past lingers in the present it defines the future.

Fuck that.

Maybe you've done some of the healing work and just have a few cobwebs to shake out. Maybe you're a hot mess of resentment, anger, fear, and reprisal and you're praying to the heavens that this book is your ticket out. Either way...or on any point in the spectrum between...I'm here to assist you in your journey to living a more authentic, peaceful, loving, abundant life. To:

- Have fewer distractions from your life's purpose and potential.
- Stop getting in your own way in relationships, both personal and professional.
- End the relationships you have with others that exist only in your head by having the courage to face your demons, living and dead.
- Contribute to your chosen profession, team, company, constituency by being clear, intentional, and healthy in your relationship to yourself and with other people.

Here's the thing: Everyone is fighting inner demons. Those demons show up through the stories that we tell ourselves about the people and situations in our lives. My job is to coach people to break free of the stories that are destroying their potential one way or another.

Unfortunately for our economy and our culture, the personal and the professional are colliding. People are riddled with anxiety, depression, and stress-related conditions. Companies are facing massive costs originating in the various forms of pain emanating from their employee base. Healthcare costs are skyrocketing, strapping companies and individuals with the financial aftermath of psychosocial issues. Chronic pain has been directly linked to trauma in childhood. When that trauma remains unresolved, it takes hold in the body in the form of various ailments and pain itself. These injured souls are fumbling through life, their false selves the only thing evident to the world. Those false selves are sufficing but not succeeding. The effect on systems can be and is often catastrophic.

Hear me now: There's *so much* on the other side of sufficing; more than the status quo. You were made for far more than average. Life demands that you break out of captivity and unleash your unique brand of awesome onto the world.

I don't blame you for wanting to stay right where you are. You're cozy, safe, and maybe you're a million miles from whatever it is that hurt you. You might not want to join me on this journey to integrate yourself, every aspect of you, including the hurt and damaged parts. It's hard to do that. It sounded downright hellacious to me, too, so I wouldn't blame you if you read this book without any plans to do anything on your end.

But I sure hope you'll reconsider.

I lead workshops that shake people out of their stuck states so they can reach for more of the joy this life offers. I teach teams and organizations how to communicate better, take accountability for their role in the messes they find themselves in, and own their own power over their destinies. Bottom line:

Because all I ever wanted was to be loved, safe, and protected, I teach people (personally and professionally, as if there's really any difference?) how to be loving, calm, and courageous.

People, I want you to direct and star in your own life. Be the hero of your own story, not the pawn in someone else's. You have the keys to your own cage so start acting like it. Unlock the motherfucker. I'm as empathetic as they come, yet my target is higher: I want you to be healthy so you can make this life matter, to make it the best it can possibly be. I see so much beauty in the world, albeit shadowed by some downright scary stuff. The only way to reduce the power and influence of the monsters is to break the cycles that were handed to us, and those that we have agreed to play out. The only way to slay a monster is to overcome your fear of it in the first place.

You've got the lock and I've got the key. Ready to get together and turn the page in your life?

~ Crazy ~

First, I have to address the elephant in the room. Okay, well maybe the elephant isn't in *your* room but he sure as heck is bumbling around, knocking stuff around in mine.

It's the *crazy*.

The crazy that I fear you'll think I'm have given the trajectory of my life to this point. That you'll judge that what I've been through makes me damaged, dirty, broken, dangerous, and, I said it, *crazy*.

As I was constructing this book, I found myself hesitating over and over again. It wasn't your typical procrastination; it sprung from deeper wells. When I finally named it, I felt a weight lift from my psyche.

When people read my stories, when they know where I came from, they will think I'm crazy and not want to work with me and they will leave me...

I mean, honestly. When I've anonymously shared even a few of these stories with people they've assumed that I'd be batshit crazy, rocking back and forth on a chair in a locked ward on meds, or turning tricks roadside with a well-loved crack pipe in my pocket. I *wouldn't* be a healthy, professional, educated woman living in the suburbs doing business with Fortune 500 companies and kickass individuals, on the road to inspiring millions.

How will they reconcile these two disparate images?

My immediate thought (as echoed by my friend, Lisa) was:

Okay, how do I move past this fear?

I know *heaps* about crazy. I was born into crazy. I was raised by crazy. I associated with and loved crazy. I hired, and was hired by, crazy. One thing I know about crazy is that crazy tends to scare the daylights out of people. You can't anticipate crazy. You can't predict crazy. Crazy is, well, *crazy*.

Me? I'm predictable. I'm not crazy. Okay, not any crazier than the rest of you all. I'm the adorable, loveable brand of crazy. We all have our moments of not making sense or acting outside of our rational mind. I happen to think that my specific brand of crazy makes me accessible, compassionate, insightful, and a whole lot of fun to work with, even when the work is heavy and hard. Irreverent, really. Some might even say I'm Rockstar Crazy.

Yet, until the drafting of this book, I had told very few people anything about these stories.

Why was that?

In all those speeches and workshops, why didn't I tell anyone about the details of my life? All these years I've alluded to the "colorful" life I've led and the "difficult" upbringing I lived through but always left it right there. Obscured from view. Why?

I didn't want to be the victim anymore. I didn't want to be the patient. I didn't want to be seen as the broken, crazy mess that I'd felt like for so long. There were years...YEARS...that I felt like I was being suffocated by sadness, hopelessness, and pain. Just living day to day overwhelmed me. For years, I suffered vivid and mind-altering flashbacks from the abuse which took a toll on my most treasured relationships, especially the one with myself. Telling people about my trauma made me feel one thing that I never ever wanted to feel again, ever.

Vulnerable.

In my experience, vulnerable was weak. Vulnerable people were prey. Vulnerable people were violated, punished, and blamed for anything and everything. To hell with that. Never again.

However, not owning these stories openly denied my essence, that of survivor. Thriver. Heroine. Badass.

Whenever I've tried to be someone who I think others want me to be, someone who they will accept, I've ended up miserable, and often alone. I guide my clients to be the best, biggest version of themselves, to take up their space in their chair, to be authentic. By daring to write this book and be vulnerable to you, I'm stepping up to that plate myself. I'm setting aside the risks of what could happen when this book is published that could rock my boat. Instead, I'm focusing on:

- The *miracles* that are poised to greet me on the other side of fear.
- The *faith* that I have in myself to make the best of every sidestep backslide.

They aren't shameful or scary unless I give them that power; that I refuse to do. Why? Because if I give them that power I allow them to hurt me not once, but over and over again. They get to control me from a million miles away, dead or alive. They aren't giving me a second thought but they dominate my own. How crazy is that? Damn crazy. I did it for *years* and *years* and all it brought me was more misery. It's how I held onto the anger and hurt they scarred me with, telling and retelling the events to myself. I had flashbacks and nightmares, all sucking me back to moments I despised living through the first time, let alone time and time again.

In writing them all down here, I can release them even further from my consciousness, sending them to the ethers and making *something good* out of *something horrible*. Offering commiseration to those who share some of my pains. Sending forgiveness to those who made some of the mistakes depicted here. Holding accountable those who have never been taken to task for their inhumane and criminal behavior. Plus, as they say in Alcoholics Anonymous:

You're only as sick as your secrets.

The passion I feel for writing this and sharing my story and insights is unmatched in my life. Ever since I saw the photo of that bruised and damaged little baby in May of 2016, I've felt compelled to bring my story to life, to give witness to the brutality hidden in the shadows of our lives. To bring hope. To offer guidance. To remind us of our blessings, even in the darkest of moments. To show you what finding your "why" is all about. This book, these stories, converge together to form my "why:" Why I expend my energy, passion, and resources into my work in the unbridled way that I do. Living through my stories gave rise to this cage rattler, thought shifter, and change strategist. The craziness, and my pain, gave birth to *me*.

~ Where Does This Crazy Feeling Come From? ~

At one tumultuous point in my life, I consulted a coach to get and keep me on a grounded path. After hearing my story, she shared a concept with me that fit me like no glove ever could. When you grow up in a crazy family with caretakers who are mentally ill, you have a tragic choice to make in order to survive.

Either you believe that *you* are crazy to think that your caretakers are ill, or, you recognize *their* illness.

If you believe the former, you trust nothing about your own perceptions, instincts, or feelings. You end up being the crazy one, which makes it easier on your caretakers because you become the problem, instead of them. You cooperate in their insanity and become a partner in perpetuating it and leaving it untreated. In that realm, you are abandoned.

The alternate choice is to believe that your caretakers are crazy. If you do, you live in a constant state of guardedness and fear because you recognize that crazy people cannot be trusted to care for themselves – or you – appropriately. If you are courageous enough to confront your caretakers and call them out on their insanity, you ensure that you will be ostracized from the family system and will take on the role of the outcast. As a child, neither of these options are safe. It is an impossible choice.

As I reflected on my own upbringing, I saw that initially I had chosen to believe that *I* was the crazy one. At some level I knew better because I did all sorts of things to help and save my parents from their own self-destruction. My focus remained, however, on me. My quest to be perfect was exhausting and painful. I thought that if only I could be better, smarter, prettier, more talented, funnier, and more loving I could change things. I thought that *I* held the key. I believed that I was the problem, because, again, I saw them as fine and me as damaged.

Over time, and perhaps by bringing myself to the brink of giving up completely on life, I attempted to change my perspective and got angry. I raged at my caretakers (which now included my step-father) and confronted them about their insanity and toxic behavior. My words were minimized and they teamed up, as unhealthy family systems do, and declared a war of sorts on me. They made me the identified patient and spoke of me like I was the damaged and crazy one.

It was so lonely. And so scary.

Because, as a child, you feel ultimately powerless to change your situation. I was tempted to regress and go back to feeling like the crazy one because it was easier somehow. But you can't turn back the clock. So, I stayed the course, and the price I paid was losing my "hero" spot in the family. I was the "problem child" instead. Being the voice of reason did not win me any popularity contests, trust me. I ended up in jail, foster care, and a mental institution before I could move out and away from them.

~ Lessons Learned ~

I'm not perfect. Far from it. The reason I'm writing this is because I've been so broken. They say the best cop is a former criminal and so it goes with me. I've been a hot flipping mess more times than I can count. I've done the polar opposite of every recommendation I now offer to you. I've been the poster child for dysfunctional thinking, behavior, and oh, how I've been thirteen shades of screwed up in my relationships, romantic and otherwise. I've learned what *not* to do so I could test drive strategies to recommend to others. My pain is your gain.

You're welcome.

There's a direct line between the work that I do and the experiences I've had.

For those of you familiar with my other body of work (personal, interpersonal, and leadership development), you're apt to recognize the origins of many of my models and approaches in the pages of this book. My techniques didn't hatch out of thin air; they emerged from my inner torment, from the pain I witnessed in and around me. I wanted to heal others, and heal myself in the process, but for many years I had no roadmap. I failed those I tried to "fix" time and time again which just deepened the pain. It was pure agony. I was swimming in it but I couldn't stay above the surface. I really believed I was drowning in it and would never survive the suffocating weight of it all.

Then I did. In these pages, I shared the pain...and the path...so you can appreciate your own even more, or perhaps discover a roadmap of your very own.

We've all had bad times, and we'll all have more. We aren't really in charge of that. I've come to realize that having bad times reminds us how precious the good times are. The gift of perspective is a precious one. When you've been to Hell and back you tend to not get thrown off track when life gets stormy. You're clear that at least it's not a tsunami and you've survived worse. This thunderstorm ain't no thing.

Insight to the rescue again.

~ **Revelations & Takeaways** ~

In case any of these didn't jump off the pages at you, here are some things I came to understand along the way.

Pain taught me how to take care of myself and urged me to do the same for others.

I'm compassionate for those with medical and mental ailments, but I also hold them to the standard of self-care. I have little time for the victim-mentality, even my own.

I struggle with a rescue mentality with people in general and men in particular. I have often felt responsible for saving others from themselves.

I developed a drive to perform, to be accepted and seen as special and loveable. I came to believe that the love that lasts longest is the love that is never returned.

I emerged from these experiences with a paralyzing fear of abandonment.

My body was violated and it's slow to forget. I thought that my body was an object that is for the pleasure of others. That my needs didn't matter.

Because I was abused, staying in the moment, showing presence and connection became counterintuitive to the dissociation that marked my life.

I spent a good, long time feeling deserving of bad, abusive treatment, holding a "bad girl" identity.

I became an adrenalin junkie. I lied, stole, and cheated at little things along the way. I wanted to have things I didn't have. I thought that if I could get my outsides to look different maybe my insides would follow suit.

I developed a strong willingness to do the work necessary to get better, to be stronger and happier.

I'm no good at whiplash, sudden changes, and people's comings and goings. Like most of us, I wrestle with my need for control and my recognition that I have very little of it.

Since I never had them, carving boundaries in relationships with others is a constant awareness and challenge.

To my detriment, I find myself being the spokesperson for others, especially when the situation involves unfairness, insanity, or abuse. Heroes attract the attention of villains.

I am acutely sensitive to criticism or any perceived rejection. Falling short in other people's eyes was downright terrifying for many years.

The anchors for my hope and healing along the way were the positive mirrors that presented themselves to me. From these people and occasions I drew energy for my recovery.

I hold a desire for calm but a penchant for chaos.

I am possessed by a drive to make this life all that it can be, holding a profound respect for its fleeting nature.

I am beautiful and special yet I am loved by people incapable of truly loving me (in healthy ways).

Angels are everywhere.

I am stronger than I often believe. I can take and overcome anything.

Everything can be reinterpreted, positively or negatively. It's all about the "facts" you pull from the story.

Everyone is made up of light and darkness. Good and evil. All characteristics are on a spectrum and all of them must be considered in context.

Giving my most to every moment is really the best I can do.

I am powerful, an old soul, and, like all of us, was given the responsibility to do something with the pains I've felt.

~ Power ~

Speaking of power...my mother used to say, "the one with more awareness has more responsibility." Armed with this book, you can welcome that awareness and claim more responsibility. Know another word for responsibility? *Power.* Want to own that for yourself?

Take some time to ponder what takeaways you have from your life, your experiences. Are they generally positive? Negative? Which ones serve you? Which ones are getting in the way of your happiness? If you could wave a magic wand and make one disappear, which one would it be? How could you challenge that assumption, to see it differently? Is there another way to see that?

Every time we hold onto a thought or an interpretation, we make a decision about how we will see the world and ourselves in it. For me, each decision pointed me toward or away from finding my true north, my healing.

In my early drafts, my best friend read a vignette and said the following: "What fascinates me is what makes one person push through to love and light like you and another person go batshit. I'm glad you chose life and love."

"Life is what you make of it" isn't just some social media meme or platitude: It's the story of my life.

"What doesn't kill you makes you stronger" isn't simply a line from a motivational tape; It's the phrase that brought me out of the darkness.

You hold the same power in your own life.

When I stopped wanting to die and chose to live, as painful as living was, I transformed my path. I gripped with bleeding knuckles the quote: "The only way out is through."

I'm offering you a guidebook for how to find that tunnel out.

~ Understanding My Path ~

This book offered another way of relating to the shit sandwiches we are often forced to eat, all in an attempt to stop the cycle of dysfunction that is destroying families, communities, organizations, and societies. They are all a bunch of intertwined systems, with individuals comprising every last one of them. Heal the individuals, heal the systems.

When individuals are locked in cages constructed by trauma, abuse, or just simple dysfunctional thinking, they wreak havoc on those around them. Hurt people hurt people, folks. Given my history, I have a somewhat unique insight into what makes people tick. I survived my early years as much as I could by studying people and determining what hurts they were harboring and what needs were driving their behavior. If I could intervene, I could save myself some heartache. I also spent a short infinity unraveling my own screwed up thinking so that I could stop living like a victim.

Now it's your turn to show up in your corner of the world in your full, bruised, battered, fearful glory. Take that risk soon – today, even – because you don't have forever. You don't even have a fraction of forever. Your life is finite, so your fear should be, too.

Honor your stories. Embrace your pain. Attend to your wounds. Then take back your power.

What power?

Your bold, loving, grateful power.

The power to define yourself however you choose. The power to bring YOU into the world in the ways only YOU can. To show up for this life with joy, even in the face of sorrow. Not in falseness, but with the wise realization that you aren't going to live forever and most of the crap you get bogged down in is a distraction from what really matters:

All that matters in this life is your experience of it and the legacy you leave behind.

What does THAT look like? Suffering and madness? Or, abundance and peace? What will you choose? Where will you exert *your* power?

One reflection I held as I wrote and discussed this book was:

This book is going to serve to continue a crucial conversation about power...and pain.

~ Power Through Pain ~

As you read in this book, I've been physically and sexually assaulted yet I refuse to wage a war against the world in response. I could and many could understand that choice given the path I've walked. Fortunately for the world, it's not that simple.

The choice is *not* between succumbing to abuse and creating more. Your power comes from choosing to move forward instead of setting up camp on toxic ground.

How can you exercise this power?

Rise above what and who has tried to destroy you. Use your power to have full dominion over your own psyche, emotions, and reactions. Serve as an example to others that *influence comes through invitation, not by force.*

For the record, I've made countless shitty choices in my life. Sometimes those choices hurt other people. I'm so sorry for the pain I've caused. So very, very sorry. I know what disabling pain feels like so knowing that I've foisted that on anyone is guilt-provoking. Whatever damage I've left in my wake, I'll tell you one thing: My shitty choices *always* hurt me.

I used to volunteer in the county jail when I lived in Virginia and was struck by the realization that we are all just one really bad choice (or several minor bad choices) away from being incarcerated. Choice defines us. This way or that way? These words or those words? This turn or that turn. Seconds and inches. A fraction of a degree off course in a sailboat is the difference between Cape Horn and Antarctica.

We are defined by our choices, big and small.

Your life is
a series of **choices**;
the most influential ones are
those that you make
in response to things
where you had
little choice in the first place.

As I persisted through these stories, I forced myself to be present with each memory. I preach from the rooftops about the power of being present, remaining in the moment. Yet, every part of my history drives me away from it, telling me to be in every moment *but* the one at hand. My survival rested in escaping the present. The present held the threat, the danger, the evil. I wanted to be anywhere but where I was.

My power sprung from wells in other moments than the present one. I've spent countless hours trapped in the fantasy of future events, crafting elaborate, movie-like scenarios in which I was adored and powerful, garnering the loving attention I so desperately desired.

The present is the enemy to the abused heart.

How did I escape the present? Music emerged as my muse. It drew my emotions forth into verse, lulling me into quiet contemplation of this fantasy life I orchestrated. It was my pain and my comfort, which were often one and the same. I sought refuge in the notes, carrying me into a space that held my truth, my sorrow, my longing. I would croon certain tunes with a passion that defied my age, making me wish that singing was my talent. I wanted nothing more than to grace stages across the country, serenading all those who had caused my heart to break into a million tiny pieces in hopes that as the words floated from my lips, I would find healing. It drove me down, and lifted me up. Unfortunately, though I was anchored in song, my mother held the lyrical talent. I mourned my lackluster skills, expressing my voice without tune in my books, my poems, and my speeches. Cream rises to the top, despite its aspirations otherwise.

Though I cannot (and would never, for your benefit) sing, I wanted to start each chapter with some song lyrics, those that symbolized that experience for me. I wanted to pay homage to those blessed with the talent to bond us together through music, a connection that carried me through many dark moments. Unfortunately, copyright rules are a bitch so I'll list my favorites here, letting you investigate the lyrics.

"Behind Blue Eyes" by The Who. *"Operator"* by Jim Croce. *"Solitaire"* by Laura Branigan. *"Secure Yourself"* by the Indigo Girls. *"Beautiful Disaster"* by Kelly Clarkson. *"Amazing Grace"* by John Newton. *"Candle in the Wind"* by Elton John. *"Harden My Heart"* by Quarterflash. *"Rise"* by Katy Perry. *"Hold On"* by Wilson Phillips. *"Rise Up"* by Andra Day. *"Dare You to Move"* by Switchfoot. *"The Angels"* or anything by Melissa Etheridge circa 1989-1991. And, of course, *"Landslide"* by Fleetwood Mac.

~ The Message in My Mess ~

I've done some pretty stupid, frivolous, and irreverent things in the course of my life, yet all of them made perfect sense when I did them. One of my very best and dearest friends has said to me, repeatedly, *"What* were you *thinking*?"* usually in response to some decision I've made about a lover, past or present. When you know me....every broken, jilted, messy, beautiful piece of me...you can comprehend what I was thinking. It all makes sense in context. It always does. For you, for me, and for every person on this planet

I h   s some tragically honest and
pai   example: To show compassion
and   who may, from the outside and
fro   rrible, insane, or ridiculous in
thei   ct of our experiences...and our
choi   . I didn't get here by accident,
but   along the way. And I'll have
many   n lucky.

I've spent my career helping people figure out their why, to connect to their true essence, to live their lives fueled by investing in what matters, to develop their strategic life plan.

To heal emotionally and spiritually.

To love and accept themselves and let the damaging forces in their lives dissipate by focusing on love and light.

To connect with themselves first so that they can connect deeply and honestly with others.

To live daringly, boldly, and authentically, appreciating the fleeting nature of this life.

In seeking to understand ourselves, we can attempt to understand others. In seeking to understand others, we can find reasons to love them. In seeking to love them, despite their misdoings, we can heal the world. We can find more peace, joy, and fulfillment in our short time on this spinning orb.

Join me?

Now I'm on a mission to empower others. It's hardly feels like a choice. I *have* to do the things I do to help others. I feel compelled to lift the veil and to take the tiger by the teeth, banishing every last monster in every head I can gain access to. When I'm in "corporate mode" I'm only able to scratch the surface. This book provides a deep dive, a more divine connection to those I serve, this time through story.

My stories have no power over me when they can no longer hurt me. I get to define my present and my future by redefining my past. Why does this matter to you? Because this means:

Your stories have no
power over *you*
when they can no
longer hurt you.
You get to define *your* present
and *your* future
by redefining *your* past.

When I found my life-changing therapist back in college, I recall telling her that I was grateful for all of the abuse. That I thanked my abusers for their treatment of me. She was not at all happy with that answer. I like to think that she was mad about that mindset because she was fearful that I was taking more responsibility for the abuse, like I always had. That I was reluctant to see them as perpetrators and me as victim by getting something useful out of it.

I saw it differently.

I saw that in them tearing into my spirit that they created a well, a well that produced a deep pain but also a deep love; it created compassion for others and their pain. In seeking to understand how I could have been preyed upon so much, I dug into the psyches of those who damaged me. In that process, I found empathy for the pain that led them to hurt me. In seeing how the pain of others damaged me, I became sensitive to how dangerous my own pain could be to others. I discovered our shared humanity. This came with dangers, of course, dangers that led me to form relationships with more abusers because I found their pain compelling; something I could fix.

I came by this honestly.

My mom believed that my dad, mom, and me were all equal players. She convinced me that I chose those horrific experiences: The abuse was a dance we danced to play out our soul lessons.

In my early twenties, I found myself in an abusive relationship. Aside from the emotional quagmire between us, one night he threw me across the room and cracked my head open but refused to take me to the hospital for fear that the child services agency would remove his daughter from our care. I sat bleeding, holding a towel to my head, blood running down my face and neck until it clotted as we ate dinner together, somehow pretending nothing was happening.

It still took me months to leave him.

When I saw the photo of that abused baby in May, 2016 I saw my own infant image in his face. I knew that I must have looked like that many times over. I imagined what the police officers must have thought when they found me hiding in that closet, covered in my and my mother's blood. The night they saw fit to remove my father from our home, to "cool off."

When he got mad, he hit. He threatened. He verbally assaulted. He raped. He shot. He killed.

My uncle stepped in the middle of them one time and my mom started screaming at my uncle telling him to mind his own business, that this was how their relationship "worked." Really, Mom?

She was the lucky one. She didn't get pitched off a bridge on Halloween 1979. That was my step-mother.

Did the abuse destroy me? It absolutely did break me, it just didn't destroy me. Like a broken plate, I could put myself back together. Now? I'm stronger in the broken places.

One thing I've learned is that the healing work is never done. It's not an item to check off a to-do list. It's perpetual. It changes form. It elevates. Sometimes there are new epiphanies that need to be worked out. One of the approaches a therapist used with me in my thirties was to speak from my voice, as a child. To see through her eyes. To apologize to her from the Universe for all the things she endured. To feel her fear, her confusion, her sorrow, her rage.

You are stronger than you think you are.

The strong can survive it – the strong can become even stronger.

~ The Most Powerful "F" Word ~

Forgiveness.

Of all the questions that I receive when I speak even in dribs and drabs about my experience, the most powerful one is "could you ever consider forgiving them?"

I could. I did. I have.

When I was growing up, I *hated* forgiveness. It was wielded as a weapon against me when I pushed against the sick system that imprisoned me. I was expected to be perpetually forgiving while they showed little mercy in knocking off their insanity in the first place. If I didn't forgive them then there was something wrong with me: It meant I was harsh, mean, cold, cruel, immature, damaged. I knew the damage they were capable of leveling me with and I saw forgiveness as a way for them to get close enough to hurt me again. To devastate me. Hell no. So I held my forgiveness deep in my spirit, refusing to part with it.

Leaving my husband poetically brought back so many wounds of my past in a way I hadn't anticipated. My mother got tied up in all of it in her patented craziness, throwing my entire life into a tailspin of excruciating familiarity. Her behavior was once again threatening my safety, and worse now, that of my children. I was in agony, twisted up inside, witnessing my past and present collide. It made me so angry, sad, and scared that I thought I might crumble.

That year, the book "The Shack" (William P. Young, 2007) found its way into my hands. I knew from all of my emotional healing work to that point that forgiveness continued to be a sticking point for me, one that I just couldn't embrace. I consumed every word of this gripping tale, expectant of its revelations, craving its healing. The author offered an explanation of forgiveness that finally gave me permission to do what my heart desired: Let go of the anger of their crimes, yet choose not to let them close enough to me to hurt me again. Up to that point, forgiveness was presented as an either-or proposition. Either I forgave them and let them back in OR I didn't forgive them and shut them out. When I realized that I could forgive them, thereby freeing myself from the burden of the resentment I held to protect and honor myself, *and still* guard against their dangerous potential by not being in a deep relationship with them, I became free.

This was truly life changing for me. It lightened my spirit. It made me the master of my own boundaries, finally. Most of all: It showed me my inner grace, a quality that had been hiding, fearful, guarded, confused, for so long.

Grace over resentment. Love over fear. Future over past. Joy over anger. Inner peace over everything.

~ Path of Suffering ~

There has been so much written on strength as a human condition, and it usually has to do with surviving some trauma or challenge. And, that's been my experience. It's not something that you're necessarily born flaunting, but when you face adversity, it may rise up and show itself. As Richard Nixon once said, "The finest steel has to go through the hottest fire."

When we are tested, we learn what we are made of. Courage comes from strength. The strength comes from knowing that what doesn't kill you makes you stronger. It comes from recognizing that you have been through as much or more as this present situation and you will prevail again.

In unnoticed suffering, one flows effortlessly into the next. It's a seamless stream of ruin, with no one and nothing to dam its influence. Healing never takes place because no attention is demanded for that end. You can't fix something that you don't admit is broken.

That is my story and explains why I found myself, time after time, in the path of abuse, manipulation, and deep despair. It found me because I was drawn to it, and no one stepped in to adjust my true north, one that mercilessly pulled me toward people that would misuse me. I mentioned this earlier: I had what people called a trauma bond. There's abundant literature on the matter, literature *I lived*. The very thing that hurt me effectively set me up to seek out more pain all on my own. Lovely.

Did my caregivers know what was happening to me? Did they just not care? For the abuse that they didn't witness first-hand, I choose to believe that we lived in a state of agreed-upon delusion where plausible deniability enforced the secrets.

When I did tell – and I did, many times – nothing happened. When it was witnessed, nothing happened. The person responsible didn't face any repercussions. It was slid under the rug.

It was as though I'd shared that someone cut me in the bus line, not physically or sexually assaulted me.

Nothing that happened to me seemed to matter much, except as it gave my mother more material for her martyred story. I was never protected or stood up for, so I grew to believe that I wasn't worthy of that. I searched for people in my life who would be my protectors, but often found bullies and abusers instead. Or, worse yet, people who would witness my poor treatment and show compassion but fail to stand up for me. That was almost worse as it left me feeling wronged yet alone.

When you grow up feeling unworthy of protection, you fail take steps to protect yourself.

For so long, I failed to see that my process of selecting people was flawed, not me. I was repeating that lonely experience over and over again until I learned that I needed to:

- Choose people better;
- Set and communicate reasonable expectations of others;
- Stop choosing certainty over suspense. Making notoriously bad choices isn't a good option, even if the perceived control makes me feel better temporarily.
- Be my own damn hero, aka, unleash my inner badass.

In other words, the way I found healing was by focusing on relationships: Mine with myself and mine with others.

Your relationship with yourself.
Your relationship with others.
They affect each other.
There is a dynamic tension
between you and everyone you touch.

Basically, these two relationship layers define who you are inside your own mind and who you share with the rest of the world.

Sometimes these are one and the same.

Sometimes you're a façade-wearing pretender who is doing a fair job fooling the world into believing you're someone you're not.

The truth reveals itself, People. Your pain is leaking out in places you might not notice and it's undermining your potential. I work with executives every day who are doing their best to play the part but the dysfunction of their companies tells a different story. If you're sick, you'll make those around you sick. If you're leading others and you're a mixed up mess on the inside, it'll show up in your organization, trust me.

Fix it. Now. Because, if not now, when? Ain't nobody got time to wait.

Mourn the sadness then move the fuck on. Be the hero of your story by writing your own ending. You may not have always held the pen, but you hold it now. You own your responses to every last thing in your life, including the stories you keep telling yourself about the world and your place in it. Rip that pen out of the hand of whoever hurt you and start crafting your own narrative. Make new meaning out of it all or you're just letting those people and things that hurt you before continue to hurt you every single day. Forever.

Wake up and refuse to give them one more ounce of your joy and peace. You owe that to yourself; you owe them nothing so stop giving them everything.

And, if you're in the singing mood, throw on Andra Day's "Rise Up" and let the inspiration fill you up.

> *"Getting over a painful experience is much like*
> *crossing monkey bars. You have to let go at some point*
> *in order to move forward." ~ C.S. Lewis*

CHAPTER EIGHTEEN
BADASS

"Let us not pray to be sheltered from dangers
but to be fearless when facing them." ~ Rabindranath Tagore

~

I love the idea about being my own damn hero, don't you?

I've wasted far too much time waiting on other people to show up in my life and take charge and sprinkle some fairy dust all over everything to make it all better.

Guess what?

It's *never* happened.

More often than not, they've ended up making it more complicated and messier.

As much as it pains me to own it, it was just another way of playing the victim in my own life. I came by it honestly: My parents trained me well. They played out their victim stories and victimized me in the process, creating another victim. I could play that out forever, understandably at some level since

I've been through so much. I was betrayed by those I was conditioned to trust. More disturbing, I was dependent upon those who were hurting me. Given that power imbalance, I had to comply in order to survive. Those coping mechanisms are a death trap when you've emerged from the original situation. Unfortunately, too many of us take that reality with us into new situations, creating a replay experience, perpetually. They victimized us then, so we stay victims forever.

Fuck that and the horse it came in on.

Part of being your own hero is owning your inner badass. It's that incorrigible person inside who wants to stir up a little trouble, stand up to the bullies, and take no shit.

Even the meekest among us can tap into the power of that inner badass, trusting that fire in our gut when we are faced with a challenge we might normally back down from.

Your inner badass is going to come in really handy as you take the reins in your own life.

Warning: Being a badass comes at a cost. The victims of the world often resent a badass and their power. Badasses confront things. Badasses don't live in the shadows and regularly draw those who do into the light. That can get ugly, but it's a beautiful form of ugly. Badassery is born of strength and love and respect.

This chapter will address that pesky relationship you have with yourself, the one that informs how you relate to everything and everyone around you. The lessons here hold the key to your life as a consummate badass.

Shall we get started?

~ Rising from the Ashes ~

There is so much pain in the world. So much destruction and conflict and anger. The violence. The wars. The unrest. The blaming, toxicity, and angst. So much anxiety and fear.

It all got me to thinking about how we might have less of all of that. More than anything, I want my life to matter. I want to make a difference and ease suffering. Although I embrace all of the gifts inherent in my *own* suffering, my life sure would have been easier without all of it. Most of it could have been avoided if others had experienced less suffering of their own. Their suffering led to mental illness (and vice versa), addiction (and self-medicating their mental illness), and grossly unhealthy means of meeting their needs.

Oooooh, needs. Yup, I said it. My first book was all about needs and how they show up in our lives and here I go talking about them again. In order to be a true badass, you need to know a thing or two about the role that needs play in your mental health and in that of others. People, and yes, that includes you, can get downright dangerous when their needs aren't being met. They are *needs* after all.

What are these needs I speak of? I recommend picking up a copy of my book, "Feed the Need," for a more thorough discussion, but I'll offer the basics here.

~ Needs and Mental Wellness ~

People have four core needs that demand to be met to varying degrees over time and circumstance.

These needs are:

- Control
- Connection/Presence
- Passion/Purpose
- Validation

The more healthy a person is, the more they are self-sufficient in getting their needs met and the more aware they are of when they are out of balance. In other words, healthy people are aware of their needs, intentional about communicating and addressing their presence, and more capable of meeting them independently and interdependently.

It follows then that unhealthy people do less or little of any of that. In my experience, unhealthy people are driven to get their needs met any way they can, to the detriment of themselves and those around them. Their needs are immense because they are in pain. We know that hurt people hurt people, typically out of a drive to get their needs met.

When I look back at my early experiences, I see so clearly how the people who hurt me were desperate to get their needs met and went about it all wrong. Clearly.

Abuse originates from a need to control and invalidate another human being, out of an effort to make them smaller than you feel and put them directly under your power. To feel in control when you feel out of control. In intimate relationships, an aberrant need for connection is served by the abuse by putting one person in control of the other, by mistaking abuse for love.

Entire libraries exist on the topic of abuse so I won't attempt to do that discussion justice here. I do, however, want you to appreciate the role of unmet needs in my story. Why? Partly to increase your understanding and compassion for those who hurt me, in hopes that this might promote prevention and intervention for someone else. When we can *see* something we can *do* something. When we can see the source of the pain we can heal it. If anyone connected to my life could have seen that all that nonsense was coming from unmet needs that might have spurred a discussion about healthy ways to get those needs met. If addiction and mental illness hadn't held the stigmas they did, perhaps treatment might have been pursued. If domestic violence hadn't been tolerated, I might have be rescued from it.

What does this mean for you, for us? It challenges us to take charge.

One requirement of opening up your inner badass is taking charge of meeting your own needs, your own mental wellness. It's taking full responsibility for your recovery from any addictions you may be flirting with, for any mental illness you may be denying. It's facing your understanding of sexual assault and domestic violence so you can be part of the conversation to end both. It's about reconciling your past with your present, perhaps using this book as your guide to let those painful stories be part of your hero journey.

If you're up for it, consider getting a therapist or a coach to team up with you on this journey. Do yourself a favor, though: Pick someone who will both mourn your pain with you *and* call you out on your shit. You want someone who will hold your hand while refusing to "yes" you death, blaming your past pain for your current problems and stopping there. Empathy is an amazing gift, but letting you swim in a shit stew is a waste of your life.

What's the pivotal factor in all of this?

The **hero** journey

is all about embracing

the power of **choice**

in everything that you

think, feel, and do.

~ Choice ~

My daughter and I were chatting one day in the car and she said out of nowhere, "I don't get it! Your childhood was hell and you're happy all the time. Nothing gets you down. He had the perfect childhood and look at him. He's miserable and angry all the time. I don't get it." My response? "Choice, Baby. You just had your first critical lesson in the power of choice."

For those of you familiar with my other publications, you know that my mind is an analytical maze. I analyze anything and everything, sorting out the options for everything from what to eat for breakfast to which business angle to pursue. Central to this game of mental gymnastics is *choice*.

We have infinite choices in any given day. Operating on auto-pilot, we pay little attention to the decisions we make throughout our lives. In terms of our mental wellness, taking charge of our choices is pivotal to our happiness and success. As I've discussed at length in my previous books, we choose our:

- Thoughts
- Feelings
- Behaviors

Our mental models about the world give rise to our thoughts and if we've been to Hell and back, our mental models can be a bit screwed up. Being a badass, we need to rattle our own cage and challenge those mental models. We can start by asking ourselves a few key questions. Think of something that's bothering you right now, some predicament that's got your attention by the short hairs. Now, ask yourself:

What thoughts, feelings, and behaviors make the most sense?

What can I live with?

How can I grow and live beyond this?

Why (or not) do I have the "right" to feel angry, hurt, vengeful?

What good will that do for me and those (people and things) I care about?

How will that empower me?

What will I be left with if I follow that path?

What if I chose another path?

Since how we see (*think* about) the world creates how we *feel* about it which then promotes how we *behave* in it, when we shift our thinking we create change in the entire series.

The more *aware* we are of this thought-feeling-behavior process the more able we are to create a space between each step. A pause.

Taking that critical moment – that pause – to reflect on a thought we are holding or an emotion we are embracing is a power move.

When we do that, we can see how much choice we have in how we think, feel, and behave and everything in our world is up for adjustment.

Wouldn't that be great? To be able to change our experience of the world for the better? To feel happier and therefore act more powerfully in our own lives? To make the most of our time on this planet? Instead of being mired in the pain of the past that we've lugged into the present, letting that shit go and living our best possible lives? I can't think of anything better. We could have a pretty amazing life and still see it as crappy, and vice versa. It's not about self-delusion, really. It's about *choice*.

Here's a little story that illustrates my point better than I ever could.

One evening an old Cherokee Indian told his grandson about a battle that goes on inside people.

He said, "My son, the battle is between two 'wolves' inside us all. One is Evil. It is anger, envy, jealousy, sorrow, regret, greed, arrogance, self-pity, guilt, resentment, inferiority, lies, false pride, superiority, and ego. The other is good. It is joy, peace, love, hope, serenity, humility, kindness, benevolence, empathy, generosity, truth, compassion and faith."

The grandson thought about it for a minute and then asked his grandfather: "Which wolf wins?"

The old Cherokee simply replied, "The one you feed."

I fed the beast of anger and sadness for years. I did my best to keep my head above the toxic waters but I submerged *so* many times. I suffocated in my own despair. Drama was my middle name because it served my need to externalize my suffering, to give it a stage, bright lights, and a large, interested audience. If I continued to nourish those demons, I'd have paid with my soul. My beautiful essence. The gift of life I was given at birth. A blessing that I squandered and lessened for too many years.

The container I chose for the stories in this book began at that birth and concluded at my defining crossroads. The moment in which I made a defining choice in my life: To choose to live, despite the pain. To do so, I walked away from a person who had abused, abandoned, and adored me, and who was slowly and surely killing me from the inside out. When I walked away, I did so with all of the rage contained in my tormented spirit for eighteen years, yet it was the only clean break I could accomplish. I saw a meme on Facebook once that encapsulated that last phone call:

Burning a bridge takes too long. I prefer explosives.

In pressing the detonation button, I extricated myself from a relationship that defined and tormented me: The one with my own father. My first abuser. One that left me dangling in the wind day after day, month after month, year after year, waiting for him to change. A day when his apologies would mean something tangible. A day when I wouldn't worry that he would slip away into the darkness without notice, without explanation.

The day I departed that relationship, I took control. I left no wonder; I was done. I wanted to live more than I wanted to love him. I wanted to learn how to love myself and he was standing squarely in my light.

I made many similar choices in the years that followed, building strength upon strength. Friends who have come to know bits and pieces of my story and the injuries I've sustained have asked me repeatedly, "how do you let it all go?"

I choose to. Over and over again. Because THAT serves me. It serves YOU to let shit go.

This book offers my talisman. My answers in the darkness. My light at the end of a long and winding tunnel of mourning....and healing.

What do I want as a result of this book?

Several things, of course.

I want you to mourn the things and people in your life that have burned you and left you with scars.

I want to inspire you to forgive them, and yourself, so that you can take back the power *you* have over your life.

I want you to find your unique message and purpose in your life, making your mess into your message.

I want you to see hope in sorrow, peace in anger, love in hate, and light in the darkness.

I want you to do these things so that, together, we can bring more beauty and grace into a world filled with pain. I'm far from perfect, yet I've fallen down and gotten up enough times that I have insight to offer to you. I can be your guide, if you'll let me.

There's a road to recovery, and you're on it.

I'll tell you one thing for sure: I wish I'd had me when I was in my cave. Then again, I suppose I did. I just couldn't see it at the time. Thanks, Me.

~ Burned by the Darkness ~

I warned you that as you took in my stories, you may have found yourself hating some of the players I depicted. Lord knows my friends and lovers over the years have held many of them in deep contempt.

Don't.

The whole point of writing this missive wasn't to burn them on a cross or wish them stoned to death. When pain begets pain, it keeps multiplying. It's the cycle of pain and injury. A cycle, by definition, is infinite. It has to be abrupted. It must stop. We are called to look after one another, not seek retribution. This life isn't about winning. It's about loving. Supporting. Healing. Injuring goes against our pure essence and runs contrary to joy.

Despite my pain and the rage it inspired, I choose joy.

Beyond that, I loved many of the people who hurt me, and with good reason. They were beautiful disasters. They were funny criminals. Well-intentioned train wrecks. Violent martyrs. Selfless narcissists. They were endlessly giving, bottomless pits of neediness, all a bunch of walking contradictions.

Like we all are.

In recognizing *their* humanity, I can forgive my own.

In the words of an old friend, we are perfectly imperfect. Flawed yet magnificent.

This is not meant to relieve them of their responsibility for their actions. *Never* that. Yet, we can still do that and continue to see them in their fullness, their good and bad qualities and choices. The worst among us still had moments of light and beauty. When we allow ourselves to embrace that truth we alleviate the anger and resentment that stands in the way of our joy. We can resist seeing things as either/or, black or white. We can also stake claim to the monsters that we sometimes allow ourselves to be, knowing that those moments need not define us. That we are more than our dark – or our shining – moments.

We are the darkness *and* the light.

We all have scratches and scars, bruises and burns. What's the difference between a person who has taken those injuries and made something good of themselves and someone who hasn't? I still grapple with some of this, for sure. One thing I can tell you is that you can use your pain as a cloak, a sword, or a light. You can use it as your excuse to hide, to hurt, or to heal. Yes, you can do all three, in any order, to a multitude of degrees, and all with good reason.

I've found that sometimes, if you haven't gotten the shit kicked out of you badly enough, you end up wounded but not broken. In addiction circles, we call it a failure to hit your rock bottom. Being injured but not shattered doesn't necessarily invite you to do what this life calls you to do in order to leave your impressive, unique, and indelible mark on it: It stops short of demanding that you be fierce.

When you've hit that rock bottom, felt the depths of pain you never thought possible, when you've had enough and don't think you can take a second more of what life is throwing at you, that's when you are called to the mat. It's do or die. Do you want to *relent* or do you want to become *fierce*?

I choose fierce every damn day.

All too often, we get stuck in searching for fairness. You've heard this before but I'll say it again: Life ain't fair. It just isn't. Bad things happen to the best and most innocent of us while good things happen to some downright evil sons of bitches. It's not for us to make sense of it. It's for us to make the best of it.

If you're reading this and you're young (young to me now means anyone under the age of 35, by the way), don't wait for a midlife crisis to wake you up to the reality of your short time on this planet. For those of you in midlife (or beyond), skip the crisis and focus on having an awakening. This book is your alarm clock. I hope to make you feel things, want things, and give things like you haven't before. I want you to wake up to your life – past, present, and future – so you don't miss it as it passes.

Whenever word of someone dying circulates I'm always darkly amused by our collective reaction. It goes something like this: "Awww, so sad. Poor so-and-so. He didn't make it." In other words, "he didn't get out of this alive." Attention, people: No one does. We spend so much time and energy missing those who have died while denying our own mortality. Death? It just IS. There's no getting around it. The timing is all that we don't know which makes it that much more pressing to let shit go and make the most of the experiences we have. To try to hold onto more love than pain.

With this book, I give you the permission to burn down the house and let the ashes rise up, bringing you right along with them. Up, high above whatever has succeeded in pulling you down.

Getting back to our mission, suffice it to say that your world revolves around you, so we're going to start at the center: Your relationship with yourself.

~ *Your Relationship With Yourself* ~

As we reviewed earlier in this chapter, the way we *think* drives the way we *feel* which informs the way we *behave*. The best way to stop a train with faulty brakes is to not let it leave the station in the first place. In people, this means challenging *assumptions* before they become *feelings* that invite you to *act* in detrimental, self-sabotaging ways. There are three critical aspects to your relationship with yourself that we need to tidy up to fuel your recovery, strength, and success:

1. Rebellion
2. Perseverance
3. Release

Step One: Rebellion

When you have shitty things happen to you and are ensconced in situations with crazy people, **rebellion** serves you well. Over the years, people have asked me how I ended up sane, happy, and not in a striped jumpsuit with weekend visitations and a parole board. With a host of answers to that question, I'll focus on the core one: I *rebelled*. I fought my way out by making it my life's mission to be different than those who hurt me. If they chose path A, I chose path B. If they went low, I rose high. If they liked math, I chose languages. I developed in opposition to my role models. They taught me, more often than not, what *not* to do.

Eventually, I made a break. I rebelled.

Make no mistake: Rebellion comes at a cost. There is protection in belonging to a group, a family unit, for example. You live by certain rules, you ignore things that may challenge the system, and you acquiesce to the needs of the group over your own needs. It's safe and comfortable. Until it's not. In my case, the costs outweighed the benefits. Some part of me grabbed onto anger in all of it, especially as it related to my mom. I let the rage rise up in me until it nearly consumed me.

That rage came out as rebellion.

I rebelled in order to survive, to gain distance from the system that was draining me of my will to live and find joy in the world. In rebelling, I provided ample reason to lose my standing with my family, my identity. In rebelling, I found myself alone.

In rebelling, I took hold of my destiny and owned every misstep along the way.

Being hit by my primary caretaker from the time I was eight weeks old set the stage for an intolerable amount of rage. Each hit, each violation, each venomous phrase squeezed my soul into an ever-compressed ball. With every hug, compliment, and encouraging sentiment, my outer layers softened, hopeful that the tightening was temporary and would be healed. By the time I reached my teens, there had been so much compression, so much burying of demons, I was a powder keg, barely capable of keeping my rage in check. I wanted to rip a hole in the atmosphere and send that toxic energy, and every memory that armed it, out into the ethers.

Please. Just. Make. It. Stop.

Let me not gloss over what this looked like. I was an intolerable wench to my family for a long time. I was cranky, defiant, dismissive, and downright rageful for a solid two years in my teens. This dissipated somewhat after I moved out when I was sixteen, but it cropped up plenty, especially with my mother.

I used the anger to create distance, a distance I needed in order to hold my truth and not feel any sort of dependence on someone I grew to know couldn't be depended on. My stepfather inherited this hot, holy mess to some extent, but his drinking and bad temper only served to bolster my certainty that no one in my house could be trusted. I don't excuse all of his behavior, but I understand that my behavior served to push him to his outer limits.

Years later, I was serving as a step-mother to a pre-teen girl, I called my stepfather in tears and asked him to forgive me for my part in everything that happened between us. I saw what that level of anger from a child could feel like as the parent trying to step in. It was painful and demoralizing, and I didn't have a drinking problem to complicate things. Although it's not found often in the initial stages, forgiveness does have a place in rebellion because it frees you from being forever tethered to the people, places, and things that hurt you.

Some things I want you to know about the path to rebellion:

- Anger is informative; it clues us in to the need for distance and separation.
- Your past informs, but does not define or predict, your future.
- Your value isn't assessed by others; that's yours to establish between you and your inner voice/higher power.

- You matter. You are not in service to others and can stand on your own.
- When you feel your own power, hold onto it. Wield it with care, but don't abuse it. Don't try to rebel against others and, in turn, become like them.
- When others fall short, feel compelled to stand tall. In other words: *Rise.*
- The stories we tell ourselves define our lives.
- Challenge the voices you hear within yourself and the ones that are around you. Just because it's said doesn't make it true. Ask yourself: Does this serve me? If not, walk or turn away from the noise.
- When you stand up to someone or something, you often get shot – or at least, knocked – down. The higher you rise, the easier the target.
- Be the love you want to see in the world.

That last one doesn't sound a bit like rebellion does it? Of all the items on that list, the last one sounds the *most* like rebellion to me. Why? Because when you've been treated badly, kicked around, and left to fend for yourself, coming from love seems like the last thing in the world you'd ever want to do. You're fifteen shades of angry, maybe even steeped in some hefty resentment. In that head space, there's no room for love. Love seeks peace. Love craves connection. Love offers forgiveness.

Rebellion from a situation that injured you opens the door to you being different than that. Being different than that means that you fixate on doing less damage, on being kinder and gentler than those who hurt you. It means that you come from love, not fear and anger.

It means that you become the love you want to see in the world. That, my friends, is the greatest challenge, and largest reward, of your life. Rebelling from the past starts with retelling your story. How? Any way you choose, remember?

~ Retelling Your Story ~

It seems that the wackier, more blessed, more unbelievable a story is, the more likely it is that I'm the one telling it. My friends share a common response to so many of my updates and announcements: "Of *course* you did." I'm *that* girl. The girl who takes risks, wears her heart on her sleeve, doesn't stop giving until it's past the point of pain. And, I love a good story. Telling a good story gives me more pleasure than the moment itself ever does. Let's tackle *your* stories, shall we?

What stories are you telling (to yourself and/or to others)?

How do these stories paint you?

Are you the hero, the victim, something else?

What if you looked at yourself as the badass in your own story? How could that change your life?

Take a story you've told a few times and pull out different parts of it than you've ever highlighted before. Realize that the details we hold create the story we tell which creates the reality we hold as truth. Just as my abusers were abusers, they were also so much more. Failing to see the grey banishes you to the extremes where growth is stunted and free-spirited joy is elusive.

Don't be that foolish.

Digging deep into the narrative that brought you to this very day can be downright ugly. The alternative is living in denial and that's an even uglier existence. I've done both so I know the tradeoffs all too well. Owning your narrative robs it of its power over you. Repeat this mantra when you need a little encouragement:

In reaching back into the dirty, I learn how to become clean.

Now, get on with it.

Step Two: Perseverance

In drafting this book, I brainstormed a bazillion titles for it. My best ideas often come as I'm driving which is quite unfortunate given the danger of journaling and driving. Nevertheless, I've been blessed enough to remember some of my brilliant musings after I come to a safe stop and can responsibly record them. One the titles I rested on for a bit was "Be Your Own Hero" because it resonated with my path to this point. I credit raw perseverance with my survival. My thriving had other sources, but there's no thriving without surviving, so thank you, **perseverance**.

Trust me, I spent many a night praying for a knight in shining armor to whisk me away and out of whatever dark hole I'd crawled into. Guess what? No such luck. I know, I know, how does a knight on horseback GET into a dark hole? They can't. I knew the way in so it follows that I knew the way out, not Mr. Knight. I held – and hold – the answers for my own path. The same holds true for you.

If you found your way in you can find your way out.

I chose the stories and timespan I did for one, clear reason: To shed light on how I got into – and out of – the darkness. At one defining moment in my life, I chose to survive. I opted to not give in. To push forward. To choose life. My life. I've chosen that path every day since.

Make no mistake: The path out of that ugly, helpless space was hard as hell. It was fraught with pain that exhausted me beyond words. At the addiction treatment center where I once worked we used to talk about how depression wasn't feeling the lowest of our lows. Instead, it was the exhaustion inherent in fighting to stay just above those depths, to *not* feel the deep feelings that threatened to break us.

I felt the fullness of every last one of those feelings. There were times I didn't think I'd see the other side of the sadness. I felt unloved, abandoned, scarred, stained, violated, you name it. I just kept feeling more of everything until I grew stronger, bit by bit, and saw that I could feel these things and not break under their weight.

I persevered.

There is nothing pretty about perseverance. It's downright ugly most of the time. It's bloody and messy and hard. On the other side of it, though, is some pretty awesome stuff. On the other side of perseverance is freedom from a past that sought to define you. There is joy even in the sadness, as you're equipped with the wisdom of knowing that life isn't best lived in shallow waters. It's hope for a better day when the sun has been hidden from view.

There are some mantras that bolstered my perseverance so I want to share them with you:

- The only way out is through.
- The body remembers what the mind forgets.
- You can depend on you, more than you think sometimes.
- Focusing on what you can be grateful for gives you spiritual fuel.
- Sometimes you just have to endure pain, disappointment, and rejection. Fighting it takes more energy than allowing it to pass through you. Everything is temporary, good and bad. Fighting the bad just ties more of your energy up in it. Part of perseverance is embracing the strength needed to allow ugly feelings to wash over you on their way out. Believe it or not, fighting the feelings and refusing to experience them just makes them stay longer and hold deeper.
- Life is worth living, no matter how tough it is at times. Allowing feelings to come and go serves you better than launching a fight against them.
- You'll find yourself "back" in familiar settings time and time again. It'll feel like déjà vu and it can really suck. Keep in mind that if you're on a path of growth and focusing on heightened awareness, intention, and peace, you'll approach each of these subsequent situations just

a little differently, a smidge more easily, and not get as emotionally triggered and exhausted.

You'll fall down but you'll get up faster each time.

An Example in Perseverance:

To survive so many traumatic moments, I dissociated from myself. I went somewhere else. One therapist in my teens said that I "intellectualized" things and that I needed to *feel* things. Hell no! Feel things? Are you kidding me? Who the fuck would want to feel the feelings connected to being beaten, raped, and abandoned repeatedly since birth? A crazy person, that's who! No, thank you. I'm all set. I'll analyze myself till the cows come home but I'm not going to re-enter my broken heart for all the tea in China. Which, by the way, I've heard is plentiful.

For this book, I heeded her counsel, bellowed a long-awaited "fuck it," and I felt it *all*. Every last waiting emotion. I crawled up into my skin and looked out through my own eyes at the world around me. Each of these stories is told from my voice, even when I was too young or too frightened to have one. In seeing the world from where I stood way back then, I can fully appreciate – and mourn – the path I've walked to present day. Every brick I've placed, every stone I've dropped, they were all in direct relationship to every other that preceded them. That's what development is all about: The selecting and refining of a path, bringing together all of your experiences into a beautiful, unique mosaic, integrating all of everything you've seen, done, thought, and felt.

I traveled this hallowed ground for you, dear reader. I want my pain to have mattered by serving a higher purpose, to be a stone in your path to healing.

Since light casts out darkness, here are some things to add light to your world:

- Add something positive to your daily routine.
- Create a gratitude journal documenting things that you are thankful for each day.
- Practice random acts of kindness.
- Each time you feel the darkness, thank it for reminding you of your strength and sit with it for a finite amount of time (5, 15, 30 minutes). Then move forward and do something kind for someone else. Take notice of the joy you bring.

From one thriver to another, trust me when I say that you can and will persevere.

Step 3: Release

Of all of the steps, this one poses the most challenges for people, myself included. We are not rewarded for our **release** of things. We are congratulated for holding on and pushing through. C'mon! I just finished telling you all about the value of perseverance!

Am I sadistic? Am I trying to confuse you?

No and no.
You can – and must – successfully do both. You must hold on and let go. You must push through and give up. Does that sound crazy? It's not. It's the sanest pitch for emotional growth I can possibly offer to you.

Perseverance actually *requires* release.

In order to move through a difficult time, whether that time is the present or a distant memory, you need to choose your battles. You must pick your poisons. You can't tackle every last thread of things that are happening or have happened. You need to release some things so the load is reasonable to bear. You need to release some of the toxic anger, resentment, and hurt that is weighing you down. You can't fly when you're encumbered by the past.

You need to let go of the darkness to hold onto the light.

Release isn't a sign of weakness, it's a sign of strength. When you release the burden of past (recent or distant) events, you reclaim your power over your present. Your arms aren't full carrying your baggage, no matter how rightful your ownership over it. You are free to select new things to touch, experience, and hold. You've been mad at those people who hurt you because they mattered, because you cared about them at some level. You had some hopes for them to be different with you. They failed you, they could fail you, because they mattered. When you don't care, they don't matter. Release allows them not to matter anymore. Ahhhhh, how good does THAT feel?

Release also means letting go of your self-contempt, for the mess you've made of things in your life. I don't care if it's your professional life, personal life, weight, health, or whatever; Stop. Say this to yourself instead:

It's no wonder why I did
such and such and ended up right here.

You are exactly where you are as a result of your prior actions and circumstances. It's an expected result of your path to this point. The only way to change the path going forward is to let go of the dysfunctional path of the past. Don't give the pain one more minute to run your life. It had your past, don't you dare give it your future!

I once shared a deep love with a man, a love that changed my life forever. Unfortunately, the relationship faced a host of challenges and it busted apart. We broke each other's hearts in the most devastating of ways, replicating our core injuries. It was devastating. We took time and space from one another and returned to see if we could find our way back to that love. Sadly, he was still so deeply hurt that he couldn't open himself up to me. His arms were full, carrying the pain of my prior departure from his life. He couldn't take my hand or hold me because he was already encumbered. There was no room for our love in his life because his space was occupied by hurt, failure, and disappointment.

Now, if he had released that pain, he might have consciously decided not to be in relationship with me again. But he couldn't get to that decision point because the hurt was clouding his reason. He couldn't make a rational decision with emotions in the way.

Lesson?

Let go of the past or it robs you of the present.

Release can also apply to things happening *in* the moment.
A client of mine was telling me about the nonsense he was facing at the office: The blame games, office politics, favoritism, incompetence. You know, a typical day at many offices. As this was going on, he was being sent for coaching, with me, to address his performance issues. He kept trying to

sell me on how unfair, inaccurate, and downright manufactured it all was, all these performance concerns lodged against him. He contemplated finding another job but he was nearing retirement and really didn't want to start over elsewhere.

Instead of focusing on his performance and how he could shift perceptions, I started elsewhere: In his narrative. Every time he exerted effort toward building his case against them, he made them the adversary. In an adversarial relationship, there is a winner and a loser (or two losers). Since that's not what he wanted since he wanted to stay employed there, I suggested that he drop the narrative. Instead of telling me, his spouse, his friends, etc. about the terrible, incompetent people he worked with and for, he was only to speak positively about them. My contention:

His narrative was creating a "him vs. them" environment, one that they could pick up on.

No one likes to be seen as stupid or incompetent and when they do, they are likely to become defensive and offensive. He was marginalizing them and they were reacting to his judgment by removing his influence. He was trying to make them feel shitty about themselves so they gave it right back to him. They had more power so he was bound to be the bigger "loser."

He made the changes I suggested and in no time, his attitude became more cooperative and insightful. His actions were aimed at building positive relationships with the people he'd previously deemed jackasses. Releasing them from his anger effectively dropped the tug-of-war between them. He cleared his review with flying colors and was able to move on from this impasse that could have cost him his retirement.

Ahhhh, sweet **release**.

Release frees us and removes the blinders so we can move intentionally and fully from one moment, one experience, one job, one relationship to the next.

A few tokens of advice on mastering this release thing:

- It serves you to let shit go.
- Exhibiting grace is preferable to demonstrating rage as it leaves you with nothing to undo or get past and gives you peace instead of resentment.
- Leave nothing unsaid; leave things peacefully whenever possible. You really don't know when that last conversation is going to take place. You may never get another chance to fix things or leave things in a good place.

~ Summary ~

Steps One, Two, and Three of owning your inner badass: Perseverance. Rebellion. Release.

The three keys to righting your relationship with yourself. Recognizing your four core needs (control, connection, passion, validation) and your responsibility for meeting them is the mark of the biggest badasses of them all. Taking charge of your thoughts, feelings, and behaviors and the choices you have and make every second of every day is how you wield the power of the badass.

Let me be clear: You are tougher than anything this life can throw at you. You were born a warrior of love. You just forgot that somewhere along the way so I am here to remind you, to challenge you, to support you, to guide you, and to inspire you to be the best version of yourself. Now. Not someday. Right fucking now. You don't have an endless supply of todays. It's prime time, Honey Badger. The story you've been living, the pages you've been turning, those are in the past. Please believe me when I say that if it doesn't serve you, burn it to the ground.

"You're a survivor because every day you make a choice not to be governed by their harsh words or actions. No one has the right to take away your happiness." ~ Assunta Harris

Rise from the ashes and
start a new story,
one that
reminds you of
your inner badass,
your hero.
You know....YOU.

CHAPTER NINETEEN
CONNECT

"Every time we impose our will on another
it is an act of violence." ~ Ghandi

~

Relationships. Connecting with other people. Bringing your big, bad self to the social arena. Before I can tackle this beauty, I have to speak to what healthy relationships are *not*. They are *not* based on trauma bonding like mine (and maybe yours) were.

~ Trauma Bonding ~

When your caretakers abuse you, especially early on in life, you're likely to develop a trauma bond. Sounds sexy, doesn't it?

It's not.

It's like Stockholm Syndrome only it defines the most central relationships of your life. According to Michael Samsel (www.abuseandrelationships.org),

"Bonding is a biological and emotional process that makes people more important to each other over time.

Trauma bonding, a term developed by Patrick Carnes, is the **misuse of fear, excitement, sexual feelings, and sexual physiology to entangle another person**. Many primary aggressors tend toward extreme behavior and risk taking, and trauma bonding is a factor in their relationships.

Strangely, growing up in an unsafe home makes later unsafe situations have more holding power. This has a biological basis beyond any cognitive learning. It is trauma in one's history that makes for trauma bonding. Because trauma causes numbing around many aspects of intimacy, traumatized people often respond positively to a dangerous person or situation because it makes them feel. It is neither rational nor irrational."

For so long, I made sense of my romantic relationships in a very Freudian way: That I was looking for a Daddy replacement. In my estimation, I had attracted withholding, angry, and sometimes cruel men because they were strong and would be able to protect me from my father. I realized that I found a bevy of former Marines in obscure places, in total disproportion with their saturation of the population.

Even after my father died, I still went for that type, thinking that I still craved that protection and safety. One day, as I was drafting this book, I stopped myself dead in my tracks when I realized that this was not the case at all. In fact, it was even more pathetic. I was looking for someone who was a great deal like my father because I wanted to be the girl they love, who is safe with them, but not because they protected me from others, but because I hoped to be special enough that I would be safe from THEM. That one little revelation...and the action required to knock that self-destructive crap off...would have saved me years of sadness, loneliness, frustration, a divorce (well, a wedding!), and a fortune. I never said I was quick.

I would spend much of the energy of my life unraveling the tendrils of his pain, fused into my body from the first time he beat me bloody when I was only eight weeks old. I was an *infant*. He was a towering biker dude, hands the size of a catcher's mitt. His rage was most often reserved for my mom, but my tears and anguish, often from witnessing him beating and raping my mom, drew his fire. He could not *stand* being laughed at or not listened to. Babies and toddlers operate off of pure emotion and that does not attend to reason. My tears sparked his rage, and the more he reacted, the more I cried. What a dangerous cycle.

Coming across a journal as I was transforming my room after a major breakup. I had written about not being able to let go. I was having a hard time moving on after a relationship. Ummmm....yup. But, why? That's a good story. My mom, my dad...if I let go of them, they would *die. They* couldn't let go. That was proof of their love and character and validation of the relationship itself. Plus, trauma-bonded people don't let go easily, especially to deep, unhealthy ties.

In mourning that relationship, I was left with a painful truth:

His lips hit harder than his fists ever could.

In the end, I'm certain that his words, those spoken and those withheld, pierced me more deeply than the physical harm he inflicted. Perhaps it's because I hold conscious memory of one more than the other. The trauma bond had taken hold on all levels, for certain. I sought out dangerous people and situations because they held the only hope for familiarity. I needed pain to feel good, as insane as that might sound. What did that get me? Oh, yeah. More pain.

Trapped in a narrative that I needed to be in a relationship with my parents, especially my mom, I chose to be connected to an open source of pain for years. The idea of "toxic relationships" hadn't hit the mainstream, though I heard plenty about toxic shame and I was swimming in it. I was angry and sad and had no healthy place to send those feelings. I suffered greatly, at my own hands.

It's clear that I had some work to do in the relationship arena. I learned a great deal along the way and because I'm nothing if not generous, I'm here to share my findings with you.

Relationships With Others

First things first: We cannot control *other people* but we can control our *contribution* to our relationships with others. As I presented in the last section, we are in charge of our thoughts, feelings, and behaviors. A simple shift in our thoughts can create massive changes in the way we feel and behave which results in transformational alterations in our world.

The three practices that will bring you calm and power in your relationships with other people are:

1. Expectations
2. Boundaries
3. Interdependence

Practice One: Expectations

Expectations are all about being grounded in the truth and not fantasy, not in what we <u>wish</u> was true.

Expectations can get us in a whole heap of trouble when they aren't properly understood. All too often, we get run over on the road of life by people who fail us in one way or another. We expect them to behave in a way that we deem reasonable, proper, appropriate, respectful, loving, etc.

Surprise! They don't. They act like the flawed, self-absorbed, fearful, irritating people that they are. That *all of us* are more often than not. The view from our high horse may be impressive but it's a load of crap. We screw up plenty yet we expect others to comply with our (often unspoken) judgments as to what the "right" thing to feel or do is.

That has failure written all over it.

Ready to live another way?

First, let's get grounded in some expectations that are reasonable to have, those I've had first-hand experience building:

- People who love you the most may hurt you the most.
- You will meet some terrible, broken people out there.
- If you don't take steps to counteract it, after experiencing pain you can be led to be the one causing pain.
- Hurt people hurt people, and you'll often find yourself in their line of fire.

Some messages I want you to keep in mind:
- Just because others treat you badly doesn't mean you deserve it.
- Waiting on someday and promises is a life wasted.
- You deserve to have standards.

- Hurt me once, shame on you; hurt me twice, shame on me.
- You are your own hero. Waiting around, putting your stock in another person to save you will leave you cold.
- Making your emotional health and happiness contingent on one relationship or outcome is foolish and squanders your potential and your joy.

Now, let's talk about one of my favorite things in the whole, wide world: *Boundaries!*

Practice Two: Boundaries

> *Boundaries are all about knowing and acting on*
> *what is okay and what is not okay,*
> *instituting your reasonable expectations and*
> *enacting consequences for violating them.*

Whether you like it or not, you are defined by the decisions you make and the company you keep. I don't mean the latter part in a reputation sort of way; I mean that the quality of your life directly corresponds to the people you hold close to you.

If I could wave a magic wand over any area of relationship dysfunction, I would choose **boundaries**. We let people cross our boundaries without even noticing that they are doing it until we are out of our ever-loving minds with irritation and resentment. We feel taken advantage of without noticing that we offered the "advantage" up on a silver platter. I grew up absolutely clueless about boundaries. Where did other people end and I begin? Nowhere. I was indistinct. I wasn't my own person. Instead, I was an instrument or receptor for other people. I lived to *serve*. I had no idea what boundaries were and

I sure as heck didn't know how to set them. I'm certain that if I had, I probably would have seen far less abuse and pain.

I would have known what hurting me looked like.

I would have known it was wrong.

I would have stayed away from people who hurt me.

I would have told them to stop when they were hurting me.

I knew none of these things because I didn't understand boundaries and saw myself as an extension of other people's needs. If they demanded something of me, it was my job to give it. My job was to fill their needs, mine be damned.

With time, and effort, comes insight.

I now know all of those things and am much more apt to call a stop to it before it gets out of hand. I did say "more apt" because I slip on this one more than I care to admit. My default position is still to give beyond reason, which, in and of itself, is not a bad thing. Giving is good. Forgetting yourself in the mix is bad. I still do that sometimes, but I'm quite conscious about it. It's like the difference between being asleep and awake in your own life. I'm awake now and am fully conscious of my boundaries. My perpetual struggle is how to hold onto them, especially when some of my triggers pop up.

What are my triggers? C'mon now, people. You have been reading this book haven't you? You're seated firmly in the deep recesses of my mind aren't you? Okay, I'll tell you. People, especially men, in need, particularly if it's me that they profess to need. It's like putting beef jerky in front of a dog. I bite, hard. I now retract faster, though, and don't get lost in it.

So, how can I help you in your own struggle?

Easy. I can help you to recognize, set, and hold boundaries.

Let's kick this off with a few non-negotiables:

- It's never okay to violate anyone or for you to be violated.
- No one has the right to hurt you or to cross your boundaries.
- In order to have your boundaries respected, you have to effectively communicate and uphold them.

And, my personal favorite and the one I'm most famous for blowing, big time:

- You can't help someone who doesn't want to be helped.

In order to know how to recognize, set, and hold boundaries, it's pretty crucial to know what they are in the first place.

Boundaries are invisible lines between you and other people. They distinguish your crazy from their crazy. They define the rules of engagement between you; what you will and won't tolerate in terms of treatment.

When someone crosses your boundaries you're likely to feel angry, sad, hurt, confused, and overwhelmed. If you aren't crystal clear on what your boundaries are, you just might not know why you feel these things. That's why it's crucial to get super cozy with those beauties so you can take back your power, and peace. How do you do that? Answer these questions and you'll be on your way.

What do you need most from other people?

What hurts you most?

What "keeps happening" in your life and relationships?

Do the people in your life know what you expect from them?

How often do they fall short?

When was the last time you sat down and renegotiated those expectations?

When was the last time you held someone calmly and clearly accountable for hurting you?

What did you learn about that relationship?

What changes, if any, to yourself and/or your relationship did you make as a result?

Beware of those people who violate your boundaries more subtly. Some people violate your boundaries slowly, like putting a frog in water and turning up the heat. The frog won't jump out and neither will you. Sudden violations are easier to see. Be mindful of those who slide over your boundary line, not just those who blow past it.

Trust your gut. If it feels icky, uncomfortable, or unsettling, pause. Attend to those feelings and look to see if a boundary just got crossed, even just a little. Those who ease across that boundary line are harder to catch but more dangerous because by the time most of us catch them, they've set a precedent that's tough to unravel. No one needs that mess, so stay on calm alert.

Setting boundaries doesn't make you an antisocial people hater. It makes you a healthy relationship holder. Now, I'll address another "how" of healthy relationships: *Interdependence.*

Practice Three: Interdependence

Once you've tackled your expectations and boundaries, it's time to examine your level of interdependence with others. Before we get started on the how, let's talk about the what. What is interdependence?

There's a spectrum of relationship connection between independence and dependence. When you're completely independent, you ask for *nothing* of others in terms of support and assistance. You look to no one for *anything*. When you're completely dependent, you rely on others for *all* of your needs. You look to others for *everything*.

In the middle of these two extremes is *interdependence*, the optimal state, where you recognize your need for others as well as your ability to rely on yourself. When you've been burned, you're apt to skedaddle over to independence, fearful of putting your stock into others. When you've been crippled emotionally, you're likely to place your emotional health at other people's feet through debilitating dependence. Though these states are understandable, it's a necessity to move through them in order to come back into balance.

Some of the tenets of an interdependent mindset are:
- We are all in this together.
- It's good to reach out for help.
- You can lean on others to the extent of their *willingness* and *ability*.
- There are angels in your midst.
- People who are supposed to care for you might not, but others will show up to take their place if you allow it.
- When others let you down, trust that you will survive.
- When they fall, you don't have to fall with them.
- When one person (or 100) messes up, it doesn't mean that humanity is doomed and you should run away.

Underneath all of this is that tricky thing called "trust." When we are fully *dependent*, we are trusting too much. When we are fully *independent*, we aren't trusting at all. In order to be intentionally *interdependent*, we need to understand how we wield trust safely. It's kind of like Goldilocks and the Three Bears and the porridge that is just right. That's what you're looking for, minus the dangerous bears.

~ Trust Muscle ~

We deserve to be saved from unnecessary hurt. The human condition naturally involves pain, but excessive pain can be mitigated by getting our **trust muscle** in shape. Yes, I said "trust muscle." Of all the muscles we have, this one gets torn and injured more than any other, especially in our fast-paced, overly-connected-yet-disconnected world. We stumble around in our relationships either rushing to judgment and handing over our trust haphazardly or we withhold it, afraid to trust other people because they might hurt us.

Working our trust muscle well helps us find a calm, powerful middle ground. It starts with one simple statement:

Trust others to be exactly who they are where they are.

People behave the way they do as a result of their experiences, mental models about those experiences, and their context. When we trust them to be who we want them to be – who we think they *should be* – instead of who they *are*, we set ourselves up to be disappointed. We're apt to use that disappointment to conclude that we can't trust other people.

Nay nay.

We absolutely *can* trust others; we just can't trust them to meet our expectations if those aren't in line with their behavior. The trust we've been breaking all of this time is our trust with *ourselves*, our judgment.

As Maya Angelou smartly stated, "People tell you who they are; believe them the first time."

The true test of the **trust muscle:**

Revamping our trust with
ourselves, to be
better judges of character,
allow others to be themselves
without feeling devastated
by their actions, and aligning
our trust with the truth
of who other people are and
what they are likely to do.

What if someone who is long gone is still taking up space in your head? What if they have taken on the role of your inner critic? How do you create a boundary for that sort of creature?

Say "thank you."

Yes, I just encouraged you to show gratitude to someone...and something...that has injured you.

Why would I do such a thing?

"Thank you" as an act of gratitude removes the power those ugly voices have over you. Fighting them just makes them fight harder to win, to overcome your objections. People, including those that live in your head, don't like to be told that they are wrong. Stop shutting them down with Stuart Smalley-type self-talk. Toss that positive affirmation crap out the window when it comes to quieting your inner critic. Make friends with it or it's going to continue to run your life.

What you resist persists.

Instead, the next time you hear the negating, insulting, critical, fearful inner voice, take a deep breath and say something like:

Thank you for reminding me
to be cautious,
to be responsible,
to offer good self-care, etc.

Then let them move on. Bless and release. Remember: Pain comes from resistance.

Now, get to work stretching and strengthening that pesky trust muscle. In the process, allow yourself to see that there is, indeed, a whole lot of good in the world.

~ Angels & Lollipop Moments ~

The other force that moved me through my journey were a series of angels, ordinary people who did extraordinary things for me, often without even noticing they were doing it.

People who provided a different mirror than the one I sought. I had a longstanding drive to be punished, to be in pain at the hands of others. When people showed me love and respect without demanding anything from me in return, they offered me another choice.

Decades later, I watched a TEDx Toronto talk on something called "Lollipop Moments." The presenter, Drew Dudley, shared a story about giving a girl a lollipop on her first day of college, making a joke about taking candy from strangers. Fast forward four years later: The young woman approached him and told him that he saved her college career by reaching out to give her that seemingly inconsequential lollipop at that important juncture in her life. He didn't remember her, but she will never forget him.

I've been the lucky recipient of many of these "lollipops" throughout my life. Together, they saved – and made – my life. In the years since they acknowledged me in these small and large ways, I've reached out to the ones I could find to thank them.

My Angels & Their Lollipops

- Being favored by sixth grade teacher, especially after beating out a smarty pants boy in a debate about bus transportation. She reflected back to me I could have a smart voice. That I could stay coherent and calm in the face of drama and excess. That I could be more capable than a boy. She reminded me of my mom, only practical, responsible, and calm.

- Being told to write this book by my grandmother, validating my journey.
- Being loved romantically as a teenager. Seen as worthy, loveable, and that I could be part of a real family.
- My college therapist and her commitment to my journey out of darkness.
- The lawyer who grieved with and for me when I was arrested after "running away."
- My high school guidance counselor and tenth grade English teacher, who both wrote college recommendations that validated my tumultuous childhood and its effect on my lackluster high school performance.
- My high school friend who gave me a pedicure when my feet were the ugliest, nastiest, driest mess you can imagine.
- My college dorm floormates who listened to all these crazy, disturbing, painful stories and assured me that I was a good, strong, beautiful person despite my scars. That I was a survivor.
- Oprah Winfrey, who faced her demons publicly, made being a survivor of trauma an acceptable identity, and gave me hope that I could make something worthwhile of my life someday, and share my story to help others.
- The stranger in Subway in Albany who approached me on his way out the door and said, "I just wanted you to know that you're the most beautiful woman I've ever seen." And promptly left, asking nothing of me in return.

Do you have a similar list? I challenge you to make one and venture out wherever possible to tell them that they made a difference. And know that every single day **you** have the chance to be on someone else's list, whether you ever learn about the affect you have or not.

~ Summary ~

Without quoting Barbra Streisand, we need other people. To survive, to thrive. To set our relationships in good working order, to maximize their positive influence in our lives, is to consider three pillars:

Expectations, Boundaries, and Interdependence.

We need to right-set our expectations about other people versus pinning our hopes to them then blaming them for their fall. Boundaries are an indicator of any healthy relationship, and are especially difficult for any survivor of abuse since abusers prey on violating them. Becoming interdependent, that midpoint along the spectrum of dependence and independence, allows us to give and receive equally in our relationships, something foreign to those of us who were raised in the wild. The power to create and sustain constructive relationships – and walking away from destructive ones – is in your hands. Remember this:

**Just because it feels like home,
it doesn't mean you should stay.**

Ready to live life large? Then let's wrap this baby up and get you on your way!

*"You either get bitter or you get better. It's that simple.
You either take what has been dealt to you
and allow it to make you a better person,
or you allow it to tear you down.
The choice does not belong to fate,
it belongs to you." ~ Josh Shipp*

CHAPTER TWENTY

FORWARD

"Heavy is the crown and yet she wears it as if it were a feather. There is strength in her heart, determination in her eyes and the will to survive resides within her soul. She is you. A warrior, a champion, a fighter, a queen." ~ r.h. Sin

~

As I start typing this first sentence of the last chapter of this book, I'm asking myself:

What did I accomplish?

The strategist in me wonders what I intended to accomplish and whether or not I missed the mark?

Here's what I wanted to do:

I wanted to stir your emotions and make you feel something, something complicated, painful, and deep.

I wanted to make you think hard about relationships, suffering, joy, and about a hundred others pieces that constitute this amazing journey we call "life."

I wanted to spur you to take action, to make changes in your life so that you could live it passionately, honestly, joyfully.

I wanted you to see how similar we all are in that we have pain, promise, good, evil, sorrow, and bliss all wrapped up in a pretty little package. That we are all crazily, magically, beautifully, really human. And to embrace how pretty damn awesome that is.

I wanted to inspire you to release the pain, resentment, and fear that holds you back from your fullest potential. To see that it's possible to not be bound to the actions of others forever.

I wanted to challenge you to offer compassion to those who are hurting you, hurting others, now seeing how hurt people hurt people. The only way to stop that is to refuse to respond with retribution and the only way to heal it is to respond with love, compassion, guidance, and release.

I wanted to encourage you to thank the pain for its lessons, its character-building opportunity, and its reminder that life is tough but you're tougher.

I wanted to remind you that your life dramatically improves when you reach for more light by letting go of the darkness, one cloud at a time.

And to remember one, crucial concept:

What you allow, you endure. So, stop it. Just stop it.

How did I do?

Since you're the only true judge of this for you, I'll leave you to it, this judging me thing. If I fall short, I request only one thing: Go back and give this book a re-read, pausing between sections and chapters to see if you're fully present in this experience, this challenge. Presence is a requirement for any good work, any true enlightenment, any lasting change.

Can I share some pretty shitty news?

The core wounds, those things that happened to you and the meaning you made out of them, leave scars that never disappear. They'll always be there, lurking in the shadows, waiting to be poked at by some trigger in present day. You'll find yourself back on the ground, dirt under your fingernails, feeling a devastating brand of déjà vu.

The good news is that you'll start to see it coming. At worst, you'll recognize the familiar feeling of being there and you'll even have a roadmap for getting back up. You'll get faster and more efficient each time. Practice doesn't make perfect in this case, but it makes it tolerable.

~

Thank you for allowing me the chance to poke around in that miraculous brain and tender heart of yours. It's been my honor to serve you.

In true Bridget fashion, I now leave you with this...a dare of the highest order.

I dare you to be the very best version of yourself.

Peace,

Dr. B.

bridget@drbridgetcooper.com

Epilogue

One of my early book reviewers asked me a couple of thoughtful questions and suggested that I answer them for all of my readers here, in the epilogue.

"How has your experience impacted your relationship with your daughters, as a parent who had no parent? How do you connect with them?"

I'm very aware of what hurt me and I've gone to great lengths to protect them. It's one of many reasons that I work from home and have cultivated a career that allows me to be there for them whenever they need me. I don't want them put in danger.

I fought for them so that they wouldn't be subjected to their father more than was required. I was clear about why I left him and how reminiscent it was for me of my early experiences and I didn't want them to grow up with crazy ideas about love and relationships and marriage.

I rarely drink in front of them. Truth be told, I rarely drink.

I lean on my friends and not on my children. For a number of years, they couldn't remember seeing me cry, which isn't necessarily a good thing. I changed that, but it's still a rare occurrence.

To this day, they don't know how I feel about their father and that's how I believe it should be. Their relationship is their relationship and I'm okay with that.

I've never had a man sleep in my bed with my kids in the house. My bedroom is not a revolving door and my kids rarely meet anyone I'm dating unless it gets serious. Even then, I carry on my romantic relationships at arms' length from my children.

I protect our mother-daughter relationship with the care that it deserves, that *they* deserve. I connect with them deeply. Every day I see how vulnerable they are so I look to protect AND equip them. I see my job as raising them to live without me.

On a positive note, I try to emulate the things I loved about my parents – the joyful playfulness, the irreverence, the spontaneity. I've tried to preserve the good and leave the bad.

Simply put, I give them the love, without the burden, that I so desperately needed.

"Let no one ever come to you
without leaving better or happier." ~ Mother Teresa

About The Author

"The secret to living well and longer is:
Eat half, walk double, laugh triple, and
love without measure." ~ Tibetian proverb

Dr. Bridget Cooper has been rattling cages since she was knee high to a grasshopper, it seems. For companies and individuals she continues that work, helping them to see the ways they imprison themselves away from the full potential of their work and their lives. She is a Change Strategist. Thought Shifter. Consciousness Raiser. She eats problems for breakfast and her appetite is voracious. She's known for being a badass, super accessible, tremendously present, and passionate advocate for clients, one and all. She inspires audiences large and small with her powerful, entertaining, and irreverent brand of connecting with others through workshops and keynote speeches. She's on a mission to change the world. How does she manage *that*?

*She guides people to be
better leaders by being better people first.*

Her drive is to help people to be clear, passionate, and invigorated about their lives and work so that they will propel themselves and their families, communities, and organizations toward success, establish stronger teams, healthy work climates, positive relationships, and happier clients and customers. Her forte is leading high-level cultural change initiatives, particularly those with longstanding conflict. She also develops and delivers custom-designed, interactive, and motivational organizational development interventions taking the form of executive strategic planning retreats and conflict interventions as well as training seminars on: effective communication, conflict resolution, relationship building, productivity, finding your passion and purpose, time management, and decision making and problem solving.

Through her education and experience, she understands relationship dynamics and approaches her work from a systemic and holistic perspective. She consults on leadership and entrepreneurial challenges for a variety of companies, and is practiced and available as a keynote speaker on any range of leadership and service topics. She provides critical advice, partnership, coaching, and facilitation for her executive leadership clientele.

She has conducted seminars, retreats, delivered keynotes, and led change initiatives for numerous associations and organizations including: United Technologies Corporation, Aetna, L-3 Communications, Girl Scouts of Connecticut, Vietnam Veterans of America, Computershare, WirelessZone, Gateway Financial Partners, The Phoenix, Junior League of Washington, Department of Defense, Allied World Assurance Company, Believe, Inspire, Grow (B.I.G.) Connecticut, CT Society of Association Executives, Glastonbury Chamber of Commerce, CT Boards of Education, Tree Care Industry Association, American Massage Therapists Association, Conference of Court Public Information Officers, CT Apartments Association, Metacon Gun Club, Women's Independence Network (WIN), CT Associated Builders & Contractors, Hartford Dental Society, Bethany College, Draeger

Medical Systems, The George Washington University, USA Weekend, Women In Business Summit, TANGO, and American Case Management Association. She ran a monthly empowerment workshop for women ("First Wednesdays"), was selected as a special guest for "Game Changers Day 2015" at Lauralton Hall and has been the featured closing keynote speaker for the Greater Hartford Women's Conference two years running.

Raised in New England, she earned her B.S. with a concentration in human resource management from the University of Massachusetts, her M.A. in marriage and family therapy at the University of Connecticut, and her Ed.D. through the educational leadership program at the George Washington University. Her dissertation was on the social network structures of women in academic medicine.

Dr. Cooper has been a leader in the Girl Scout organization, President of the Parent-Teacher Organization, soccer coach, religious education instructor, and elementary school room parent and activity chairperson. Prior to her move to Connecticut, she served as an instructor in conflict resolution and anger management for inmates of the Fairfax County Adult Detention Center. Her hobbies include traveling to places far and wide and seeking out photo opportunities of people, places, and things. She has a never-ending bucket list that she's slowly checking off, and she takes suggestions.

She has four other books aimed at assisting organizations and individuals solve their personal and interpersonal challenges.

"Power Play," her fourth book and 2016 bestseller, provides a roadmap for reducing the culture killers of stress, drama, and isolation that are draining organizations, communities, and systems of all shapes and sizes.

Her third book, "Stuck U.," guides readers through her five-step change process at the individual and organizational level, shedding light on the core competencies that make or break change initiatives.

"Feed The Need" (2014), her first book, will change the way you think about problems, and strengthen and empower you to solve them. In this groundbreaking book, you will discover how to identify, understand, and feed your core emotional needs so that you can live more harmoniously with yourself and others and resolve any conflict more effectively. She adapted this guide for teenagers in "Feed The Need: Teen Edition" (2014), with a foreword written by an inspiring high school student.

Please contact her to gain her insight and partnership on solving your personal, professional, and organizational challenges at bridget@drbridgetcooper.com or by visiting her website at www.drbridgetcooper.com.

"If everyone were cast in the same mold, there would be no such thing as beauty." ~ Charles Darwin

Quotations

I kept my voice central in this book but found it difficult to do so since I love to weave quotes in to solidify and illustrate my thoughts. Our collective voices are so much more powerful than just one individual's. To me, seeing our innermost musings in a stranger's words signifies that we are not alone in our experiences. The pages that follow hold the quotes that I originally inserted in this manuscript and extracted out upon final review. Enjoy. ☺

~

"There is no greater agony than bearing an untold story inside you." ~ Maya Angelou

"The world is violent and mercurial – it will have its way with you. We are saved only by love – love for each other and the love that we pour into the art we feel compelled to share: being a parent; being a writer; being a painter; being a friend. We live in a perpetually burning building, and what we must save from it, all the time, it love." ~ Tennessee Williams

"What is true meditation? Being awake and alive to this precious moment." ~ Jeff Foster

"Turn your wounds into wisdom." ~ Oprah Winfrey

"Life is brutal. But it's also beautiful. Brutifal, I like to call it. Life's brutal and beautiful are woven together so tightly that they can't be separated. Reject the brutal, reject the beauty. So now I embrace both, and I live well and hard and real." ~ Glennon Doyle Melton

"Be a lamp, a lifeboat, a ladder. Help someone's soul heal. Walk out of your house like a shepherd." ~ Rumi

"It takes a lot of courage to release the familiar and seemingly secure, to embrace the new. But there is no real security in what is no longer meaningful. There is more security in the adventurous and exciting, for in movement there is life, and in change there is power." ~ Alan Cohen

"Life is a journey. Death is a return to earth. The universe is like an inn. The passing years are like dust. Regard this phantom world as a star at dawn, a bubble in a stream, a flash of lightning in a summer cloud, a flickering lamp – a phantom – and a dream." ~ Vairacchedika 32

"Our lives begin to end the day we become silent about things that matter." ~ Martin Luther King, Jr.

"The difference between living and feeling alive is using your fear as fuel to fly." ~ India Arie

"The greater a child's terror, and the earlier it is experienced, the harder it becomes to develop a strong and healthy sense of self." ~ Nathaniel Branden

"You are free to choose, but you are not free to alter the consequences of your decisions." ~ Ezra Taft Benson

"You have to participate relentlessly in the manifestation of your own blessings." ~ Elizabeth Gilbert

"I am lessons learned and have yet to learn. I am wisdom still in route to finding knowledge. I am seasons of brokenness always renewing wholeness. Every day is a new day to become more."
~ Kayil Crow

"Until you heal the wounds of your past, you are going to bleed. You can bandage the bleeding with food, with alcohol, with drugs, with work, with cigarettes, with sex; But eventually, it will all ooze through and stain your life. You must find the strength to open the core of the pain that is holding you in your past, the memories, and make peace with them." ~Iyanla Vanzant

"Never let yesterday use up too much of today." ~ Will Rogers

"I think that because this is a moral universe, then right will prevail, goodness will prevail, compassion will prevail, laughter will prevail, love, caring, sharing will prevail. Because we are made for goodness. We are made for love." ~ Desmond Tutu

"It's not what you look at that matters. It's what you see."
~ Henry David Thoreau

"Adversity has the effect of eliciting talents, which in prosperous circumstances would have lain dormant." ~ Horace

"Damaged people understand that every evil demon that exists down there was once a kind angel before it fell." ~ Nikita Gill

"If you want to change the world, go home and love your family."
~ Mother Teresa

"Every experience, no matter how bad it seems, holds within it a blessing of some kind. The goal is to find it." ~ Buddha

"Love is how you stay alive, even after you are gone." ~ Mitch Albom

How We Rise Up From Our Pain

"We are shaped by our thoughts; we become what we think. When the mind is pure, joy follows like a shadow that never leaves." ~ Buddha

"Sometimes you get the best light from a burning bridge." ~ Don Henley

"And, most surprising of all, that I could carry it. That I could bear the unbearable." ~ Cheryl Strayed

"Forever is composed of nows." ~ Emily Dickinson

"I am not looking to escape my darkness, I am learning to love myself there." ~ Rune Lazuli

"Only those who will risk going too far can possibly find out how far one can go." ~ T. S. Eliot

"Always seek out the seed of triumph in every adversity."
~ Og Mandino

"If there is no wind, row." ~ Latin Proverb

"I went into the bookstore and asked the saleswoman, 'Where's the self-help section?' She said if she told me it would defeat the purpose." ~ George Carlin

"The walls we build around us to keep sadness out also keeps out the joy." ~ Jim Rohn

"Adversity causes some men to break; others to break records."
~ William Arthur Ward

"A sufi holy man was asked what forgiveness is. He said, 'It is the fragrance that flowers give when they are crushed.'" ~ Rumi

"People say walking on water is a miracle, but to me walking peacefully on earth is the real miracle." ~ Thich Nhat Hanh

"What you do makes a difference and you have to decide what kind of difference you want to make." ~ Dr. Jane Goodall

"Act like what you do makes a difference. It does." ~ Henry James

"The most common way people give up their power is by thinking they don't have any." ~ Alice Walker

"Oh, soul, you worry too much. You have seen your own strength. You have seen your own beauty. You have seen your golden wings. Why do you worry?" ~ Rumi

"The best gift you are ever going to give someone: the permission to feel safe in their own skin. To feel worthy. To feel like they are enough." ~ Hannah Brencher

"These mountains that you are carrying, you were only supposed to climb." ~ Najwa Zebian

"Always remember you have within you the strength, the patience, and the passion to reach for the stars to touch the world." ~ Harriet Tubman

"Always forgive your enemies. Nothing annoys them so much." ~ Oscar Wilde

"They say time heals all wounds. I disagree. The wounds remain. Time, the mind protecting its sanity, covers them with some scar tissue and the pain lessens, but it is never gone." ~ Rose Kennedy
"They tried to bury us. They didn't know we were seeds." ~ Mexican Proverb

How We Rise Up From Our Pain

"If you are willing to look at another person's behavior toward you as a reflection of the state of their relationship with themselves rather than a statement about your value as a person, then you will, over a period of time, cease to react at all."
~ Yogi Bhajan

"If your nerve deny you, go above your nerve." ~ Emily Dickinson

"Sometimes our light goes out but is blown into flame by another human being. Each of us owes deepest thanks to those who have rekindled this light." ~ Albert Schweitzer

"And though she be but little she is fierce." ~ Shakespeare

"Abusive parents have inappropriate expectations of their children, with a reversal of dependence needs. Parents treat an abused child as if the child were older than the parents. A parent often turns to the child for reassurance, nurturing, comfort, and protection and expects a loving response."
~ Benjamin James Sadock

"Soon you realize that many people will love the idea of you but will lack the maturity to handle the reality of you."
~ Reyna Biddy

"Don't ask for a light load, but rather ask for a strong back."
~ Anonymous

"Do not go gentle into that good night; rage, rage against the dying of the light." ~ Dylan Thomas

"When sleeping women wake, mountains move." ~ Chinese Proverb

"At every moment of our lives, we all have one foot in a fairy tale and the other in the abyss." ~ Paulo Coelho

"I find a rapture linked with each despair. Well worth the price of anguish. I detect more good than evil in humanity. Love lights more fires than hate extinguishes, and men grow better as the world grows old." ~ Ella Wheeler Wilcox

"Life becomes easier when you learn to accept the apology you never got." ~ R. Brault

"Impossible is just a big word thrown around by small men who find it easier to live in the world they've been given than to explore the power they have to change it. Impossible is not a fact. It's an opinion. Impossible is not a declaration. It's a dare. Impossible is potential. Impossible is temporary. Impossible is nothing." ~ Muhammed Ali

"My wish for you is that you continue. Continue to be who you are, to astonish a mean world with your acts of kindness." ~ Maya Angelou

"I have decided to stick with love. Hate is too great a burden to bear." ~ Dr. Martin Luther King, Jr.

"I love when people that have been through hell walk out of the flames carrying buckets of water for those still consumed by the fire." ~ Stephanie Sparkles

"We already live on the planet of war, we already live on the red planet, and it's a war against children. All the other wars are just the shadows of the war on children." ~ Stefan Molyneux

"By developing a contaminated, stigmatized identity, the child victim takes the evil of the abuser into herself and thereby preserves her primary attachments to her parents. Because the inner sense of badness preserves a relationship, it is not readily given up even after the abuse has stopped." ~ Judith Lewis Herman

"I learned that courage was not the absence of fear, but the triumph over it." ~ Nelson Mandela

"There are generally three parties to child abuse: the abused, the abuser and the bystander." ~ Louise Penny

"There's only one way to avoid criticism: Do nothing; say nothing; and be nothing." ~ Aristotle

"Why not go out on a limb? That's where the fruit is." ~ Mark Twain

"All the adversity I've had in my life, all my troubles and obstacles, have strengthened me. You may not realize it when it happens, but a kick in the teeth may be the best thing in the world for you." ~ Walt Disney

"Sometimes the hardest person to walk away from is the person you've always assumed you were." ~ J.M. Storm

"Children who experience abuse also learn to deny pain and chaos or accept them as normal and proper. They learn that their feelings were wrong or didn't matter. They learn to focus on immediate survival - on not getting abused, and miss out on important developmental stages. As a result, they have problems developing their own identities." ~ Randi Kreger

"You will either step forward into growth or you will step back into safety." ~ Abraham Maslow

"Alice: How long is forever? White Rabbit: Sometimes just one second." ~ Lewis Carroll

I'd also include "And Still I Rise" (1978) and "Why the Caged Bird Sings" (1969) by Maya Angelou but, those, too, are copyrighted. I recommend that you read them. Over and over and over again.

Made in the USA
Charleston, SC
19 February 2017